SST™

SST™

Successful Selling to Type

Dr. Arnold Tilden

LD

Library of Congress Number:		00-191654
ISBN #:	Hardcover	0-7388-3072-0
	Softcover	0-7388-3073-9

This book was printed in the United States of America.

To order additional copies of this book, contact:

Xlibris Corporation

1-888-7-XLIBRIS

www.Xlibris.com

Orders@Xlibris.com

CONTENTS

Acknowledgements 11

Introduction 13

I: The Evolution of SST™ 17

The MBTI

Make it and Sell it

Counseling to Type

Selling to Type

Balance and Shade

A Trusted Adviser

The Final Nudge

SST Highlights

The SST Five Point Foundation

The Logo

SST in Ten Words

II: SST Tools 27

Industry Profiles

Behavioral Cues

Implications of the Four - Part Framework

III: The Investigation 31

A Crucial Skill

Rackham the Revolutionary

Easy to Comprehend, Hard to Do

An Ironic Obstacle

Line of Investigation

Steps to Developing a Line of Investigation

Don't Forget to Practice

Tilden's Line of Investigation

Objections: A Symptom of Ailing Investigation Skills

Summary

IV: Four Languages of SST 47

Taking in Information

Organizing and Deciding

V: STs: The Stabilizers 50
ISTJ
ISTP
ESTP
ESTJ
VI: SFs: The Cooperators 60
ISFJ
ISFP
ESFP
ESFJ
VII: NFs: The Catalysts 70
INFJ
INFP
ENFP
ENFJ
VIII: NTs: The Visionaries 81
INTJ
INTP
ENTP
ENTJ
IX: Four Buyer Influences 92
Balance & Shade
Economic Buyers
User Buyers
Technical Advisers
Wins, Results & SST
X: Sales Success Formula 99
Sales Performance = Skills X Motivation
Skills
Motivation
XI: The Evolution of Selling 104
The World isn't Flat (June 1997)
Counseling & Selling (August 1997)
Listening (October 1999)
What's wrong with one guy's opinion? (March 1999)
Duh (November 1998)

XII: SST in Practice 112

What distinguishes SST (October 1997)
SST & SPIN: A Paradox (October 1997)
SST & Four Buyer Influences (December 1997)
Preparing Holiday Turkeys (November 1998)
Selling malpractice (March 1999)
Avoiding the FAB Trap (July 1998)
Sighted squirrels find more nuts (March 1998)
What if Willie Loman, Blake & Lou Gehrig had Power Point? (May 1999)
Rethinking the sales force (May 1999)
Balance and Shade (April 2000)
Ron Cherry: My friend & mentor (April 2000)

XIII: Sales Leadership 138

Lombardi on Leadership (February 2000)
Sales management diagnosis (September 1998)
Dangling carrots (September 1998)
Paradox II: Soft skills make a hard difference (January 1999)
Silver Bullets (September 1998)
Kirkpatrick's Model (July 1998)

XIV: The SST Practice Tee 156

Questioning
Listening
Balance & Shade
Implementing SST
SST Training

References 169

To my father Arnold Sr., a retired career sales person, who started every workday with a predawn commute to Manhattan. From him I learned to love work and the discipline it requires to succeed. To my mother, Elaine, who taught me to love language.

3-TILD

Acknowledgements

I would like to acknowledge my friends, family and business associates for, not only reviewing the manuscript for this book, but for their ongoing support and guidance with SST. After all, it has become an intellectual child.

First, the late Ron Cherry was my friend and mentor who served as the catalyst to my consulting career. Ron was just the brightest guy I've known.

Russ Brooks has been a trusted adviser in the development of SST, critiquing the original binder and co-delivering the earliest workshops. SST is organic in nature and Russ continues to provide guidance and support in its ongoing development.

Inge Olson helped design the logo and put together a very effective website at www.tildensst.com. She has assisted with oversubscribed workshops and been a continuous source of support.

My daughter Rachael Tilden has done the most careful editing of the manuscript. This is the same Rachael who some twenty years ago tried to improve what she perceived to be a boring dissertation by coloring most of the pages. Today, Rachael is a graduate student in counseling who did a stint in sales and thereby brings a unique perspective in critiquing SST. As you will learn, SST applies counseling principles to selling.

Finally, my PfP partner Harry Koolen and I were fraternity brothers at St. Lawrence University and worked together as houseboys (washing dishes in exchange for board at a sorority house) before we had even heard of "Permission Marketing." Harry recognized the power of SST at a reunion which led to renewing a friendship and launching a business partnership. SST is often an important component of the work we do with PfP clients.

Introduction

When people ask, "What do you do?" I sometimes wish I were a fireman, accountant, teacher or any other occupation that basically describes what you do in a word or two. Instead, I will offer, "Sales Education" as my field. "Oh, you're a sales trainer", they often reply.

At this point, I bite my tongue to prevent me from carrying on about the differences between "training" (for dogs) and "education" (for people).

My less direct reply is that, "I have developed a personality based sales education program we call SST for Successful Selling to Type."

If this elicits, "Oh, you're one of those motivational speakers like they use at Mary Kay conventions" I have learned that the most prudent course is to just give up.

More typically, however, the conversation turns to the short version of how our program helps people communicate more effectively by customizing messages to the preferences of prospects and clients.

This book is intended for everyone who has said or, at this juncture is thinking something like: "Sounds great. But, how do you do it?"

Chapter One describes the "Evolution of SST" and how it has grown from the recognition that counseling and selling require the same basic skills of: asking good questions, listening and helping clients choose solutions.

Chapter Two, "SST Tools", introduces essential and necessary tools to sell successfully to type. They are Industry Profiles, Behavioral Cues and Implications of the Four Part Framework.

Chapter Three is devoted to "The Investigation". Without good questions and listening there can be no SST.

Chapter Four, "The Four Languages of SST", covers how each of us combines a preference for "taking in information" with one for "organizing and deciding" that determines one of four natural orientations for thinking. Once we know our own preferences, we can be more effective communicators by "balancing" messages we send to ensure that they appeal to all types. When we know the preferences of the person we are communicating with, we can "shade" the messages we send in that direction. Balance and Shade are core SST concepts.

It is important to emphasize that while **Chapter Five through Eight** profile sixteen personality types (Four for each language of ST, SF, NF & NT) the real thrust of SST is to better understand one personality: your own. With an improved self-understanding you can "balance" your messages to appeal to all types.

SST is an eclectic approach integrating principles of personality theory with two other consultative selling approaches. The first is Neil Rackham's SPIN Selling approach with which we deal in Chapter Three. **Chapter Nine** develops the other, Miller & Heiman's Buyer Influences model.

Chapter Ten proposes our "Sales Success Formula" which is Performance = Motivation X Skills. It can be a very helpful diagnostic tool both for understanding the dynamics of individual performers as well as those at a team level. It is also an important reminder that, just because you have acquired great skills from SST, doesn't mean you can ignore the daily disciplines that are influenced by the "Motivation" part of the equation. The formula is multiplicative which suggests that a wonderfully skilled person with zero motivation to succeed will deliver zero level performance.

SST is organic and continues to evolve and improve as it is applied in the field. We reinforce its growth and the skills of its practitioners with a bi-monthly newsletter. Archived articles from "SST Newsletter" serve as the content for **Chapters Eleven through Thirteen.** Respectively, they address issues associated with: The Evolution of Selling; SST in Practice and Sales Leadership.

Chapter Fourteen, The SST Practice Tee is for those of you who want to close the gap from "knowing" to "doing". There are no real secrets. Practice is the key and this chapter provides a few drills to help you convert what you learn in SST to improved performance.

For those of you looking for the "real short" version of SST, we illustrate it in just **ten words** below:

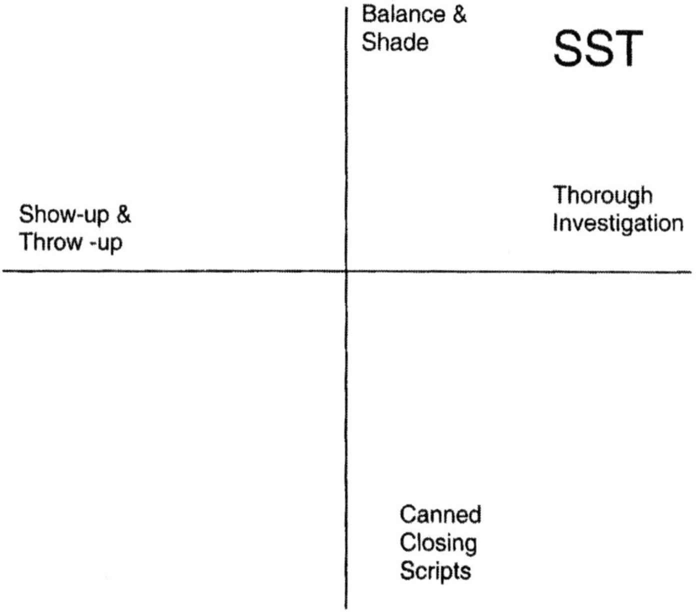

Balance & Shade

SST

Show-up & Throw -up

Thorough Investigation

Canned Closing Scripts

CHAPTER I

The Evolution of SST™

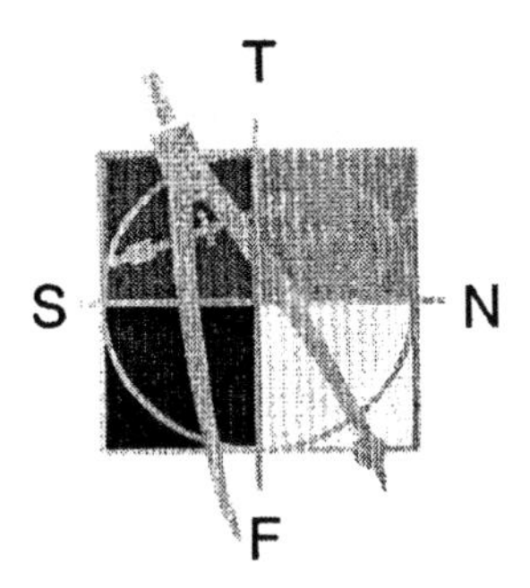

In the early 1990s a faculty colleague, Ron Cherry, invited me to help a consulting client of his improve teamwork through the use of the Myers Briggs Type Indicator (MBTI). At the time, I was teaching psychological testing and assisting Ron with his innovative approach to teaching management skills to undergraduates. TQM, or Total Quality Management, was taking off and long time hierarchical organizations were seeking to flatten their structures and catch-up with the Japanese. That introduction to consulting was the impetus to my career transition and the development of SST, a selling relative to the MBTI.

The MBTI

The MBTI is the world's leading personality inventory and has been completed by millions of people since its inception in the 1940s. It is based on Carl Jung's theory of personality types and enables its users to determine natural preferences for "thinking" and "communicating". The Jungian model, upon which both the MBTI and SST are built, is illustrated in Table 1. Jung's theory holds that each of us has a natural preference for one behavior over the other on each scale. The pattern of those four preferences identifies a personality type that is often communicated by a four-letter code. Mine is ENTP, or Extraverted Intuitive Thinking Perceiver.

Table 1
The Four-Part Model

	Where we prefer to do our thinking	
Extraversion E		Introversion I
	How we prefer to take in information: Perceiving	
Sensing S		Intuition N
	How we prefer to organize and decide: Judging	
Thinking T		Feeling F
	Get it settled (Judging) or Get more information (Perceiving)	
Judging J		Perceiving P

Like to Know Your Type?

If this is your introduction to type theory and you would like to have a "preliminary hypothesis" of what your type might be, using the Behavioral Cues tool illustrated in Table 3 of Chapter 2 will be a good exercise. Simply place a check mark adjacent to the phrases that sound like you and tally them for each of the four scales. A fuller understanding of your "true type" would require participation in a program like SST.

Make it and Sell it

Business theories can become quite elaborate. But, fundamentally, starting a business enterprise comes down to two prerequisites. You must be able to:

1. Make it
2. Sell it

Given the success Ron Cherry and I enjoyed helping clients realize their teamwork objectives, I was confident in our ability to deliver effective consulting. In other words, we could "make it". However, the question of being able to "sell it" was still an untested proposition.

This prompted an investigation of what the state of the art was in selling. Remember this was the early 1990s, when the internet was in its infancy and before there was an Amazon.com. When I resorted to the low-tech means of visiting business section of bookstores, most titles I found were by the likes of Zig Ziglar and Tom Hopkins. I read both authors and was left with the sense, to be kind, that the body of selling literature was pretty shallow stuff.

Further, when I contemplated applying the Hopkins and Ziglar "methods" on real life sales calls I was completely uncomfortable. Their tactics were both manipulative and transparent. Prospects were (and still are by too many) viewed as adversaries to be overcome with clever closing scripts by those with enough testosterone to use them. Even worse, they don't work in the kind of selling I was doing with sophisticated buyers who were looking to make pretty healthy investments to correct complex problems.

Counseling to Type

Instead of using popular methods, I naturally gravitated to communication skills I had learned and used as a professional counselor.

1. I asked good questions
2. I listened carefully
3. Once I demonstrated understanding, I helped the client choose a solution

When I reached the third level, what Steven Covey has called seeking to be understood, I relied on principles of "Counseling to Type". In this approach counselors are influenced by research (Yeakey, 1984) indicating that their effectiveness improves when they use the communication style of their client instead of their own. For example, an "Extraverted" career counselor might assume that the best way for a client to gather career information would be to "network". That is, of course, unless the client happens to have an "Introverted" orientation. To an "Introverted" client the sound of "networking" can be like running fingernails across a blackboard. In "Counseling to Type", the counselor, regardless of his or her own preferences, would offer "Introverted" clients options that would allow them to process information in a private space like library research or computerized career interaction software.

Selling to Type

My personal application of "Counseling to Type" skills to selling proved powerfully successful. I planned and asked good questions and listened attentively to responses. Once the problem was sufficiently understood, I customized the proposal to the preferences of the client. Sensors were taken step-by-step with lots of practical details and specifics. Conversely, Intuitives were given the big picture first with an emphasis on competitive advantages.

My entrepreneurial compass started to turn in the direction of introducing a selling process to teach people to "sell to type". Could sales people learn and apply counseling skills? Could they learn to recognize personality preferences? What if they couldn't type someone during a sales call?

Eventually the answer came to me: It didn't matter.

What does matter in communicating to type, whether it be in a counseling or selling setting, is the recognition of our own preferences and our tendencies to send messages to others the way we, not they, would like to receive them. Put another way, benefiting from SST does not require an extensive understanding of sixteen personality types. There can be a tremendous value gain in communication effectiveness from a better understanding of *<u>one</u>* *personality type; our own.*

Balance & Shade

Teaching sales people, or anyone else for that matter, their Jungian personality preferences is a snap. And, once our preferences for communicating are recognized and understood, it is not difficult for people to learn to "balance" their messages. For me, this principle means to be careful to incorporate Sensing and Feeling themes to balance my natural Intuitive and Thinking tendencies.

Just "balancing" messages increases communication effectiveness. But, most people scream their preferences to us and it is usually easy to identify Jungian type. When we are clear on someone's preferences, we can "shade" our communication toward them. This means giving Sensors lots of facts and details up front and filling in big picture implications later. On the other hand, when we know we have an Intuitive, we lead with the big picture and keep the facts concise. A more extensive treatment of "Balance & Shade" appears in Chapter Eleven (P. 131) under a SST Newsletter archived article of the same title.

A Trusted Adviser

Having sorted out the question of whether or not "selling to type" was a teachable concept, and being Extraverted in character myself, I was anxious to find a sounding board for what was still an embryonic idea. When I asked around for a good thinker on selling, one who might even combine a practical and academic perspective on the process, the name Russ Brooks kept surfacing. At the time, Russ was senior vice president for a very successful community bank and teaching selling in Penn State's Smeal College of Business.

Russ' enthusiasm for a "selling to type" model burst through his "Introverted" veneer. He reinforced my sense that existing selling models were based on work "hard" instead of work "smart" kinds of assumptions. Further, like many other executives, he had been introduced to Carl Jung's theory through a bank supported MBTI program. He found it to be a useful model in understanding his "Intuitive" preferences in a "Sensing" dominated industry.

Russ has been a trusted adviser in the development of SST. He critiqued each page of the "SST Binder" before it was submitted for copyrighting. In fact, we delivered the test run of SST to Russ' former employer, Nittany Office Equipment in State College.

The Final Nudge

The final nudge to pursue the "Selling to Type" idea full bore, came from my attendance at a Tom Hopkins seminar in 1994. Prior to Hopkins, the last time I had experienced comparable pedagogy was in elementary school. Remember the workbooks where you filled in missing words in sentences? Well, the ones below were lifted directly from the workbook I received at the Hopkins workshop. (Tom Hopkins: Low Profile Selling, 1994, P.4)

"John, Mary, I so appreciate your allowing me to ________ with you today. I'm thrilled to offer you the exciting ___________ of benefiting from the (your product or service) like so many others." (The answers: "visit" and "opportunity")

The Hopkins program was a mix of memorizing scripts, strategy *("If you are showing a house with a damp basement, warm-up some cinnamon rolls in the oven to cover up the odor")* and motivation.

Here's an illustration of a Hopkins motivational technique, a daily "chant" for the shower. These words appear on a device designed to hook over a showerhead:

*"I'm alive! I'm awake! And, I feel great! I feel good! I feel fine! I feel this way all the time!" (*And, I'm not kidding*)*

Of special interest to me was the Hopkins treatment of personality types. He offers a one-sentence description for "six personality types of buyers" (Tom Hopkins: Low Profile Selling, 1994, P.6)*:*

"Believing Bart, Evasive Ed, Griping Greg, Anna List and Domineering Donna."

Want to guess how many people were in attendance in Harrisburg, Pennsylvania that winter day? An estimated 1500. Hopkins was scheduled the next day in Philadelphia for an even larger crowd.

The Hopkins encounter left little doubt that:

1. There was a market of people interesting learning about this fascinating process called selling
2. The early notions of "Selling to Type" were far more sophisticated

SST Highlights

Fortified by the genius of Carl Jung and driven by the market opportunity, we rolled SST out in 1994. Here are a few highlights in our brief history:

- SST was a key ingredient in enabling a regional advertising sales office to move from "near the bottom" to the top national producer
- In a field study with an experimental group using SST and a control group without it, new sales went up by 483% over a four-month period for those using SST. Performance for the control group remained flat.
- Using SST, an information technology firm hit their annual sales target after the second quarter

ILD

- SST has been successfully applied in a wide array of industries including: advertising, employee benefits, banking, investment management, insurance, HVAC engineering and services, architecture, law, accounting, industrial lighting, real estate and information technology.
- Dackheden Human Management Consulting AB, a Swedish Consulting firm working with some of the largest clients in Scandinavia, has been certified to sell and deliver SST in Europe. See "SST for Scandinavia" in Chapter IX, SST in Practice.
- Dackheden Human Management found us at tildensst.com our web site that was designed by Inge M. Olson in 1997
- The www.tildensst.com site is where the bi-monthly SST Newsletter is published. Archived newsletter articles serve as the principal source of readings for this text.
- A class reunion at St. Lawrence University prompted a dialogue with classmate, fraternity brother and fellow "house-boy" Harry Koolen. With synergy in the air we formed a strategic partnership with PfP Consulting, Inc. Through that alliance, SST has been introduced to marquee financial services accounts like: First Union, Barclays Global Investors and Credit Suisse First Boston.
- We have formed a strategic alliance with I-SYS Technologies to join forces to help businesses improve sales performance. Our end will be to ensure that clients have the appropriate sales methodology and skills in place. I-SYS will deliver expertise in automating the system with SalesLogix technology.

The SST Five Point Foundation

1. People are different
2. Jung's theory is a proven framework for understanding similarities and differences

3. We tend to sell to (and manage) others the way we prefer to be sold to (or managed)
4. Sales performance increases when we are able to communicate to others in their preferred style
5. Sending messages that are balanced and appeal to all preferences increases sales performance

Latin Motto

Influenced perhaps by too many years in academia, we felt for a while that SST needed a Latin motto. Then, like a bolt out of the blue, it came to us when a client (Mike Morruci, sales manager for Penn State Geisinger Health Plan) observed, "The real lesson of SST is that *it is not about you. It is about them.*"

Russ Brooks had a faculty acquaintance in Penn State's languages department translate Mike's musing. Thus, the formal SST Motto is:

Non de nobis agitur. Sed de istis

It is not about you. It is about them

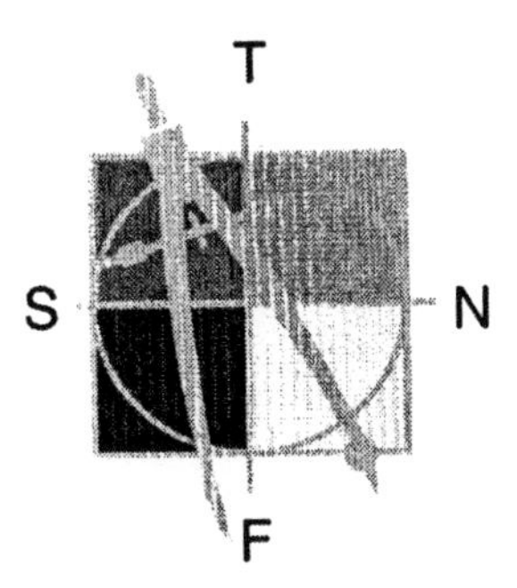

The Logo: SST™ is anchored in Carl Jung's theory of personality types and applies the combinations of mental functions to identify four distinctive ways of thinking and communicating. The four languages are represented as colors and comprise the four quadrants of the logo: ST Stabilizers (green); SF Cooperators (red); NF Catalysts (yellow) and NT Visionaries (blue). SST™ provides steps and tools to first determine preferences and then to improve communication with both clients and team members. Section D of the workbook is color-coded and profiles each personality type you will encounter in selling. The compass symbolizes the SST tools enabling its practitioners to identify and communicate in the preferred style of the client.

CHAPTER II

SST Tools

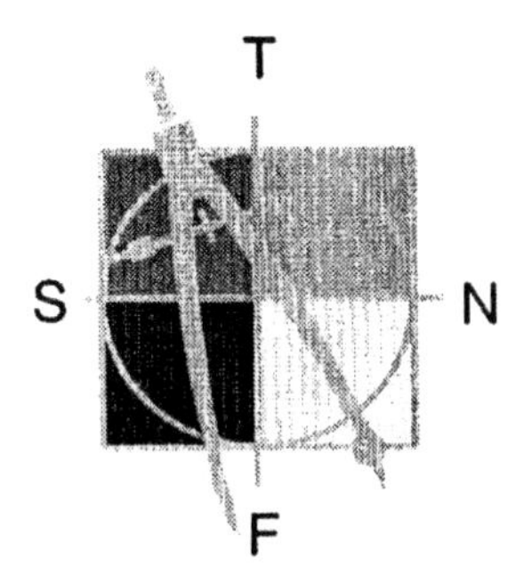

Although there have been crazier ideas, we don't initiate the SST process by asking prospects or clients to complete a Myers Briggs Type Indicator to enable us to sell to their type. Instead, we rely on two basic SST tools: "Industry Profiles" and "Behavioral Cues".

Industry Profiles: Birds of a Feather Flock Together

The former is based on voluminous research that has been conducted with the MBTI to determine personality patterns in various occupational fields. The Center for the Application of Personality Type (CAPT) in Gainesville, Florida has been a clearinghouse for research on personality type and occupations and serves as the source for "Industry Profiles". One of the distinguishing characteristics of SST, one that sets it apart from other personality based selling models, is the research that supports it.

Knowing a prospect's position or academic background, and referring to Industry Profiles in Table 2, can provide us with a "working hypothesis" of his or her preferences. For example, if we are calling on a CFO who is also CPA, we know there is a strong probability that we will encounter a Sensing-Thinking, or ST personality type. Conversely, the human resources person in attendance will most likely have an Intuitive-Feeling or NF set of preferences.

Table 2
Industry Profiles

Stabilizers	Cooperators	Catalysts	Visionaries
ST	SF	NF	NT
Accounting	Teaching	Counseling	Law
Engineering	Health Care	Human Services	Physical Science
Banking	Social Work	Music	Higher Education
Business	Religious Work	Art	Architecture
Law Enforcement		Behavioral Science	Research

The source for this table is Atlas of Type Tables Macdaid and others, CAPT, 1986

Industry Profiles is a summary of a handful of occupations that provides a representative sense of how Jung's theory verifies what our every day experiences indicate to us: birds of a feather tend to flock together. We are also able to draw upon the many volumes of research that have been submitted to and stored by CAPT on hundreds of other occupational fields and customize profiles for the kinds of clients and prospects you encounter.

Behavioral Cues

A key term in Jungian theory and SST is "preference". Just as we are born with a natural preference to use a right or left hand, so to are we born with preferences for how we think and communicate. When you get dressed in the morning, do you put your left or right leg in your pants first? Imagine putting your non-preferred leg in first. You can do it and you will get better with practice. But, you will feel awkward and uncomfortable.

Similarly, when we are required to use our non-preferred thinking style, it feels unnatural and requires lots of concentration. Conversely, thinking and communicating in our preferred mode feels natural and easy. Our preferences manifest themselves in our behavior. In SST, we use "Behavioral Cues" illustrated below to gauge the preferences of our clients or prospects.

Table 3
Behavioral Cues
How did your prospect behave during the investigation?

Extraverts (E)	Introverts (I)
- Readily discusses things	- Appear to think it over before talking
- Offer opinions	- Ask thoughtful questions
- Appear open	- Appear private
- Welcome interruptions	- Dislike interruptions
- Appear ready to act	- Appear to want to think it over.
- Seem to have a short attention span	- Concentrate for a long time.
- Talk it out	- Think it through
Sensors (S)	**Intuitives (N)**
- Want facts	- Want "Big Picture"
- Want "Tried & True"	- Want "Cutting Edge"
- Ask for references	- Consider possibilities
- Observant	- Imaginative
- Ask for figures	- Anticipate your words
- Want to do it "right"	- Show interest in doing it differently
- Go step-by-step	- Make an Intuitive leap
Thinkers (T)	**Feelers (F**
- Focus on ideas	- Focus on people
- Act "business like"	- Convey personal interest in you
- Point out a flaw	- Behave tactfully
- Want logical reasons to buy	- Want to promote harmony
- Perform calculations	- Forecast reactions of others
- Appear firm but fair	- Appear warm & enthusiastic
- Seem objective	- Seem sensitive
Judgers (J)	**Perceivers (P)**
- Seem more decisive than curious	- Seem more curious than decisive
- Want to get it settled	- Want to leave it open
- Seem to have things 'under-control'	- Seem involved in many projects
- Have a tidy working area	- Have a not so tidy working area.
- Seem orderly	- Seem flexible
- 'The way it ought to be'	- 'The way it could be'
- Self regimented	- Spontaneous

"Behavioral Cues" can be used with clients you have met for the first time, those you know well, and all of those in between. Our strong recommendation, however, is that you never type during a call itself. During those precious minutes it is crucial to stay in the moment, to listen empathically and to genuinely devote yourself to understanding the client and his or her issues. The communication process we want to pursue with SST is a dialogue, not an interrogation.

Once the call has concluded, and as soon thereafter as possible, "Behavioral Cues" should be used to record your impressions and to advance your SST hypotheses.

Beyond the Golden Rule
Implications of the Four-Part Framework

While "Industry Profiles" and "Behavioral Cues" are tools to help us read the preferences of prospects and clients, "Implications of the Four Part Framework" serves as an outline of how to communicate effectively with others. We can use it go beyond the Golden Rule of, "Do unto others as you would have them do unto you." The SST Communication Rule is, "Communicate with others the way they, not I, prefer."

Table 4
Implications of the Four-Part Framework

To be most effective in communicating with them, I should...

Extraverts (E)
* Allow them to "think out loud"
* Demonstrate enthusiasm
* "Do - Think - Do"
* Expect them to throw ideas out & see what sticks

Introverts (I)
* Allow them to ponder privately
* Demonstrate respect for their privacy
* "Think - Do - Think"
* Expect them to conceal reactions

Sensors (S)
* Give facts, figures and details
* Be prepared to give bottom line quickly
* Be practical and describe past successes
* Propose in the context of building on what they do now
* Proceed step - by - step

Intuitives (N)
* Paint "big picture" and possibilities
* Be concise with details
* Describe future benefits
* Highlight cutting edge
* Accommodate "intuitive leaps"

Thinkers (T)
* Be logical
* Emphasize your competency
* Be well organized
* Itemize costs & benefits
* Persuade with logic

Feelers (F)
* Be friendly
* Show that you care
* Positive impact of your proposal on people
* Positive difference" for people as a benefit
* Persuade with enthusiasm

Judgers (J)
* Expect them to offer a time frame
* Observe it.
* Be prepared for a quick answer
* Don't surprise them with changes

Perceivers (P)
* Offer a time frame
* Don't be offended if they don't observe it
* Allow for changes and extensions
* Expect changes

Chapter III

The Investigation

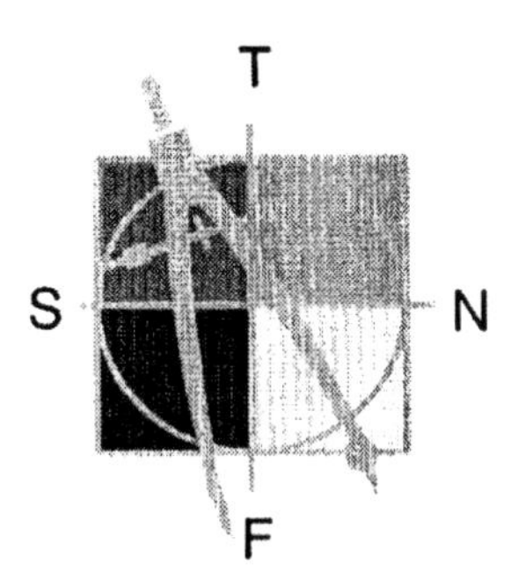

A Crucial Skill

To begin, we should make it clear that we use the terms "Investigation", "Discovery" and "Needs Assessment" pretty much interchangeably. The process refers to the essential selling skills of asking good questions and listening to understand your client. Without good questioning and listening skills, there can be no way of customizing communication to the preferences of prospects and clients. In other words, without a thorough investigation there can be no SST.

To demonstrate how crucial investigating skills are to consultative selling, we often conduct an exercise during SST where we ask participants to prepare for an appointment as though they were a counselor on a college campus. (This is also described in the "Selling Malpractice" newsletter article in Chapter Twelve). Little information is given other than the student, who had a good first semester, starts missing classes regularly and the first round of exams shows the inevitable nosedive in grades. A faculty member calls and schedules an appointment for the troubled student with you.

LD

Without exception, participants plan excellent questions for the exercise. They would learn as much as possible about the student before the appointment. They seek to establish rapport with the first level of questions. Multiple hypotheses are explored. Excellent attending skills would be demonstrated.

The "Moral of the Story" is quite transparent as the exercise is processed. That same level of preparation and attention to questioning and listening they propose for the case is, by their own admission, rarely demonstrated when calling on clients and prospects for sales. Too often, salespeople show up for a call and start pitching FAB, or Features, Advantages and Benefits. We have termed a call where the salesperson just pitches and doesn't investigate the "Show-up and Throw-up" approach.

When we research clients and ask what aggravates them the most about sales people, we consistently hear responses like:

"They don't listen."

"They only show–up when they have something new to pitch whether its something we need or not."

"They never take the time to understand what is distinctive about us."

Rackham the Revolutionary

Neil Rackham deserves considerable credit for focusing attention on the investigation process. In fact, we can even say that Rackham helped revolutionize the selling field. When he launched his monumental research (SPIN Selling, 1988), the best companies in the world (IBM, GTE, Xerox, Exxon, Kodak etc.) were teaching a selling approach that emphasized skills like "closing" and "handling objections".

Clients started telling Rackham that, while closing and handling objections seemed to work in lower order sales, those same techniques rarely succeeded in higher value selling. These conversations (and a $1 million dollar bank roll) prompted Rackham and his team to launch what turned out to be a twelve-year study of what works in selling. They investigated 35,000 calls. Just to let the weight of that number sink in we'll write it again: 35,000.

Rackham's empirical findings supported the central point made above: "closing" and "handling objections" showed no empirical relationship to succeeding in major and complex (e.g. multiple buyers) settings. Neither did asking "open-ended "questions.

If those traditional manipulative techniques don't work, what does? Rackham's findings were clear and compelling: What did distinguish exemplary performers in major account sales was their skill at asking good questions.

"There is a clear statistical association between the use of questions and the success of the interaction. The more you ask questions, the more successful the interaction is likely to be." (Rackham, 1988, P.14)

The reception to Rackham's research, at least initially, was anything but warm. It was hard for Fortune 100 companies to come to terms with the fact that they were teaching the wrong skills. Ten years ago Rackham was a heretic. Today, his research supporting the importance of asking good questions is embraced by every sales organization serious about consultative selling.

Easy to Comprehend, Hard to Do

The evidence is clear. Successful sellers with major accounts ask questions. You can even plan them in advance and write them down to ensure that you are asking the right kinds of questions. In fact, you should plan them in advance and write them down. Although it sounds easy, we have found that it is not.

It is difficult for those of us, particularly Extraverts if you will, to garner the patience and discipline to ask questions and listen. Each time there is a window of airtime we want to fill it with our story laced with FAB. The reasons are psychological and sociological and beyond the scope of this endeavor. Suffice it to say that most of us would rather talk than listen.

An Ironic Obstacle

When we have helped sales forces make the major conversion from "selling by telling" to "question and listen first", we often encounter an ironic obstacle in the road to consultative selling. It is how Rackham's SPIN system itself has been implemented.

While we are great admirers of Rackham's research and writings, we take a different path in developing effective questioning and listening skills than a strict SPIN process. Too often, we have found clients who are disenchanted with their investment and efforts in teaching and learning SPIN. The problems fall into the following categories: Too Prescriptive; Lose Client Focus; Too Uncomfortable; The Problem Dump.

Too Prescriptive. Our research and experience have both shown that many practitioners find the SPIN system overly prescriptive. Many sales people collapse under the weight of recalling the ratios of Implication to Problem questions, for example. Others ask one good question and prospects (those Extraverts again) proceed to answer twenty other questions. Trying to be diligent in learning a new skill, the sales person proceeds to ask all the questions he or she has planned anyway.

Lose Client Focus. Another common problem is that people become so focused on the questions they are asking that they forget to listen to the client. While the client is describing a significant problem the interviewer is racing through his notes wondering which question to ask next. *Have I asked all of my Problem questions? Would that be an Implication or Need-Payoff? What does Need-Payoff mean again?* Planning and asking a sensational question that isn't joined with effective listening is a wasted exercise.

Too Uncomfortable. Another difficulty we find when clients are struggling with the SPIN program is that they are not comfortable asking some of the questions. For example, they might think that a "Need Pay-Off" like, "Why would you find this solution useful?" is painfully obvious. They would feel insulted if someone asked them, and therefore feel uncomfortable asking others. The result is an awkward moment in the dialogue, where the interviewer is ambivalent over management's expectations and the sheer discomfort of fulfilling them.

The Problem Dump. Finally, there's the "Problem Dump". Too many make the mistake of assuming that the investigation is a linear process. They assume it will follow Rackham's SPIN steps in order. In reality, prospects and clients will often dump a pile of problems on the table all at once.

The investigation rarely looks like this:

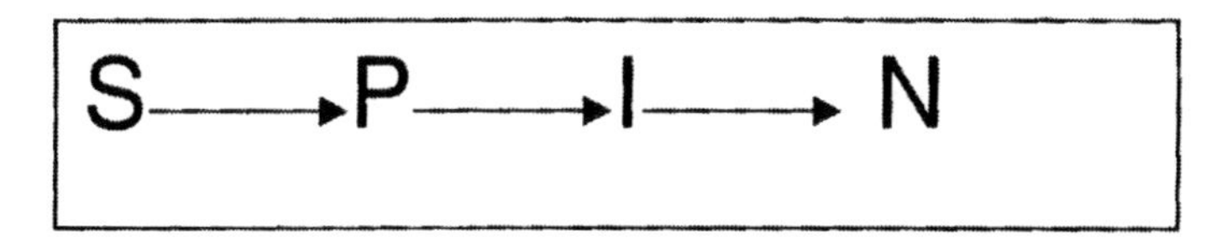

We find weak investigators taking just the first problem they hear and walking it through the subsequent questions in the SPIN model. This is tantamount to leaving gold on the table.

The artful investigator will take each and every problem and learn as much as possible about it, the consequences to the business and what a solution might mean. The investigation often looks like this:

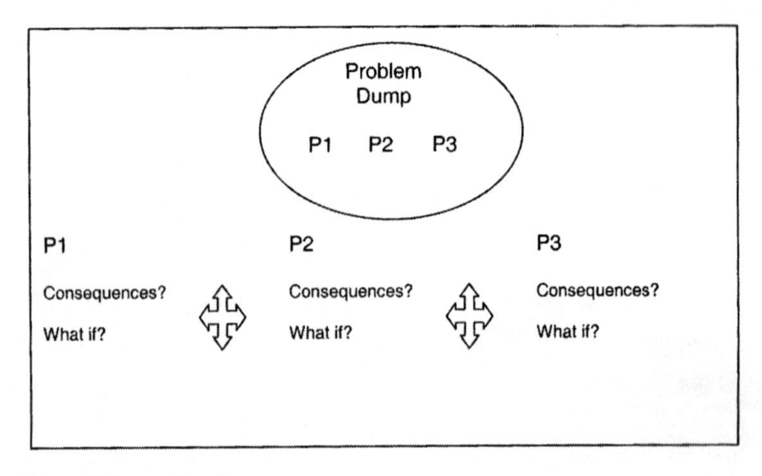

Line of Investigation

We refer to our approach as developing a "Line of Investigation". While it is influenced by SPIN and we are deeply appreciative of Rackham's research, a "Line of Investigation" is different in a number of important ways.

Dialogue is Preeminent. A "Line of Investigation" never appears or feels like an interrogation. It promotes a "dialogue" where there is a give-and-take that flows between the prospect and he interviewer. Isaacs, (1999, P. 19) defines "dialogue" as "a conversation in which people think together in a relationship".

With a "Line of Investigation" interviewers should feel free to contribute helpful anecdotes, evidence and the like that reinforces relevant points in a conversational style. Too strict SPIN interviewers act like Dragnet's Joe Friday who want "just the facts" in a one sided interrogation.

Comfort is Crucial. The objectives of the investigation are basically twofold: One is to learn as much as possible about the prospect and his or her business problems. Two, is to start to build a relationship where the client is comfortable with you as a solution provider. If you are not comfortable during the interview it will show.

Anytime we learn something new we can expect some level of discomfort. But, if you think a question is really stupid, don't ask it. Find another that accomplishes the same objective.

Shut-up and Listen. Remember: A great question planned and asked is a wasted exercise without listening. Instead of listening, most of us want to "reload" with our next comment or question. (See SST Newsletter article on "Listening", p. 131)

At the risk of offending some, the best investigation advice we have given many clients is to simply "shut-up and listen". One of the reasons the Introverts among us often excel at selling is that they are better listeners. While many Extraverts make the mistake of thinking "Selling is Telling", Introverts are doing what comes more naturally to them: listening.

Memorize it. Don't worry, we are not asking you to memorize something long and difficult. A "Line of Investigation" is really a guide to a give-and-take dialogue. All you need to memorize is a short list of the problems you typically find with prospects and clients. Each time you uncover one you follow it with your favorite "Consequences" and "What if" questions that are described in the next section.

Partner Harry Koolen often dramatizes our training sessions by playing the "Sales Manager from Hell."

"Now, I'm the Sales Manager from Hell (as he dons the hat embroidered with SMFH). I call you at home at 3 am and ask for your "Line of Investigation". What do you say?"

Be ready for that call.

Steps to Developing a "Line of Investigation"

There are three parts to golf: 1.) The grip 2.) The stance 3.) The swing. Sound easy? Ask anyone who plays the game and they will tell you that it can be simultaneously the most rewarding and the most frustrating game they have ever tried. No one will tell you that it is easy.

Similarly, we can assert that there are just three steps to developing a "Line of Investigation": 1.) Study the categories of questions offered below 2.) Choose questions from each that are a good fit with you 3.) Practice.

Because there are just three steps does not mean it is easy. There are times when it might even be a little bit frustrating. But, we can assure you that it will be time and effort that will be well rewarded as you develop an essential SST skill.

The first two steps are to review the questions listed below and to choose the ones that are a best fit. Rackham's work heavily influences the categories of questions we list. His SPIN process stands for: Situation Problem Implication and Need-payoff questions. The acronym, he acknowledges, is forced and the term "Need-Payoff" just isn't a good mnemonic helper. While we couldn't do any better with mnemonics, we did choose terms that are more descriptive of the category of questions. We substitute "Fact" for "Situation" and "What would it mean if.." for "Need Pay-off".

Questions of Fact

<u>Definition</u>. Ask for <u>facts</u> about prospects current situation

Comments.

- Least powerful line of questions

- Get answers to as many as possible prior to first face-to-face,
- www is a great resource
- When you can, show that you have done your homework
- "I read about the recent acquisition of ABC on line. What will that mean . . .?"
- If you ask too many questions seeking facts, the buyer can get bored
- Keep preliminaries brief.
- Research shows that major account buyers want you to get down to business before too long

Examples.

- What do you have?
- How many?
- How long?
- What is important to your customers/clients/staff?
- Why do they choose you?

Problem Questions

Definition. Probes to uncover problems or needs

Comments.

- Focus on the client rather then your product or service.
- Prospects rarely see you unless they have a problem or need.
- Skilled questions uncover problems and needs
- Asking about and acknowledging what they like often facilitates the transition to what they don't like.
- The fuller your understanding of the problem and need, the larger the solution.
- "Typical" performers ask about problems and then present solutions

LD

- Larger solutions lead to larger sales
- Resist the FAB Trap (See archived newsletter article: "Avoiding the FAB Trap", p. 123)

Examples.

- What works well with your current. . . .?
- What would you like to see improved?

Consequences

Definition. Asks about the consequences of a problem or unfulfilled need

Comments.

- Research shows that this is the most powerful question form
- It is also the most difficult to ask
- "Exemplary" performers ask questions about consequences
- For each problem you uncover, follow up with a probe about consequences
- The investigation rarely unfolds in a linear fashion
- Multiple problems and needs often get dumped out in one pile
- The art is pulling them out one-by-one and fully learning about the consequences of each
- The better you are at learning consequences, the fewer the objections when you propose solutions
- Prospective clients almost always know their problems and needs
- However, they are often exploring and learning about their consequences for the first time through a skilled investigation

Examples.

- When that problem occurs what are the consequences?
- Walk me through the last time the problem occurred
- What happens if you don't fix it?
- What impact does it have on other parts of the organization?
- Have you ever assigned a dollar amount to it?

What would it mean if you. . . .?

Definition: Asks about the value gained to a solution

Comments.

- These questions make the transition from problems to solutions
- Put a "happy face" on the problem solved or need fulfilled
- You begin to look at problems as a "consultant" from the same side of the desk rather than a "sales rep" across the desk
- The prospect often starts a conversation about your solution
- Let them talk

Examples.

- What would it mean if you could solve the problem?

Don't Forget Step Three: Practice

The only way to get comfortable with a new line of investigation is to practice. Recruit family and colleagues. Ask them to play the role of a prospect as best they can. Deliver your "Line of Investigation" and ask them what they thought and felt about each question. Did you make good transitions from "Facts" to "Problems" to "Consequences" to "What if"? Did you put them at ease? Anything you did particularly well? Would they target places for you to improve? Did they feel that you were listening carefully?

Tilden's Line of Investigation

Practicing what we preach, I start with Questions of Fact. I look to demonstrate that I've done my homework by prefacing a question with something like, "When I visited your website, I was intrigued to learn about your recent acquisition. How's the merger of the two sales forces going?"

One of my favorite questions is to ask, "Why do your clients choose you?" Responses can be a terrific indicator of their type preferences. Basically, they will tell you what you need to do to be chosen by them.

After covering all the questions of "Fact", I move to "Problems" by asking what they like in their sales force. The key transitional question is, "What would you like to see improved?" They wouldn't be talking with me unless there was some improvement they thought we might help bring about. This is likely true of your sales calls as well. As Alec Baldwin observes in David Mamet's memorable movie, Glengarry GlenRoss, "A guy don't walk on the lot lest he want to buy." (For those familiar with the film, you will understand that civility prohibits me from any other Glengarry quotes.)

Once we move into "Problems" I'm listening real carefully and sometimes writing furiously. This is especially true if I'm encountering a "Problem Dump". I associate dollars with every problem I hear. The more the merrier. As they say in golf, "Every shot makes somebody happy."

Identifying problems is the key to selling solutions. I am always prepared to prime the "problem pump" with a few zingers. My questioning on "Exemplary Performers" usually comes first.

Question: *"I assume you have some Exemplary Performers or Stars. They are people who consistently hit or surpass their targets. Have you ever analyzed what they do that sets them apart?*

Typical Answer: *They build personal relationships with clients*

Follow up: *What do you do to help "Typical Performers" build relationships with clients?*

Typical Answer: *We don't*

Question: *What proportion of your sales force is performing at the level where you would like them to be?*

Typical Answer: *I have never had a prospect indicate a proportion higher than 60%.*

I continue to probe areas that I know are sources of frustration to those executives managing or leading sales teams.

Question: *Do your "Typical Performers" get trapped selling on price?*

Typical Answer: *"Too much. They go to price quickly when we want to sell value."*

Follow up: *Do your Exemplary Performer sell value?*

Typical Answer: *Our stars are able to build relationships and sell value."*

Follow up: *Do you teach what your Exemplary Performers do well?*

Typical Answer: *No*

Another favorite problem question I like to ask is about lost business.

Question: *Have you ever lost a deal when you had a superior product because the competition outsold you?*

Typical Answer: *Drives us batty*

LD

Basically, if the "Sales Manager From Hell" called at 3 am and asked me to offer my Line of Investigation it would go like this:

- Why do your clients choose you?
- What do you like now? What don't you like?
- Got some stars?
    - What do they do?
    - Do you teach the other what your stars do?
- Typical performers get trapped selling price?
    - Stars sell value?
    - Do you teach the other what your stars do?
- Lose any deals when you had superior quality?
    - Got outsold?
    - How often?
    - How much?
- What would it mean if a greater proportion of your sales force demonstrated the kinds of skills your Exemplary Performers demonstrate?

Objections: A Symptom of Ailing Investigation Skills

Right after "close them hard and often" the second most common old school selling bromide was and, for too many still is, "handling objections". Our research and experience consistently show that the more thorough your investigation, the less probable it is that you will have objections to handle. If you find you are dealing with objections on a regular basis it may be that you are pitching solutions before you have thoroughly understood the prospect's problems. Therefore, our focus in SST is to consider objections as a symptom of an investigation ailment rather than a clever tactic to coerce a "close".

Monitoring how many and the types of objections you are handling is a good measure of how effective you are at the investigation's twin skills of asking good questions and listening. The more you get the more room you have for improvement. Further, if you consistently get a similar kind of objection it usually points to an important value area that you have neglected to develop in the investigation. Depending on whether your investigation ailment is one (volume) the other (specific) or both, Dr. Tilden has different prescriptions.

Diagnosis. Before we can make a good prescription, we need good data to diagnose. When you debrief a call jot down the kinds of objections, if any, that surfaced. If you are a sales leader, this is a good exercise for you to ask everyone to do. You can use it diagnostically to help develop investigation skills for individual team members or on a team-wide basis.

Volume. If you find a high volume of wide ranging objections it very likely suggests that you, pardon the expression, are "showing up and throwing up". Dr. Tilden's prescription for this ailment is to read this chapter twice more and to call me in the morning.

Specific. If, however, you are able to isolate the category or categories of objections you are fielding we have a different prescription. Anticipate the objection with a question.

When we work directly with clients, we will ask them to isolate objection categories. Not surprisingly, "price" is a common objection category. Typically this is a symptom of not building value by investigating to learn the prospects problems and matching a solution. Too often, we see solutions being pitched that add no value for this client. Remember: *"Non de nobis agitur. Sed de istis."* It is not about you. It is about them.

An experience we had with a manufacturing client should serve as a good illustration of how to anticipate an objection. Our client manufactures an engineering solution that is much smaller than what is commonly in use. Their product enables their clients to make smaller and sleeker looking products. Smaller and sleeker holds great value implications for end users.

Prior to SST, our client's sales team would show–up, pitch FAB and then wait for objections that were almost always about price. Our prescription was to anticipate the objection with questions like:

"Are your end users interested in smaller technology?"
"What kinds of things would smaller technology enable them to do?"
"Is sleeker design important to end users?"
"Does the "packaging" influence how end users buy?"
"Is design an important consideration in your strategy?"
"Would a smaller. . . . . . solution provide more design alternatives?"
"What would a smaller. . . . mean for your strategy"
"What would a smaller. . . . mean for your marketing objectives?

The results of using this line of investigation were terrific. Objections went down. Prospects were articulating the value proposition before it was pitched. And, as they say, the crowd went wild.

Remember the question in my "Line of Investigation" dealing with typical performers getting stuck on price? Exemplary Performers who sell on value ask questions like the ones posed above to build value. Be an Exemplary Performer.

Summary

Everyone in sales owes Neil Rackham a royal debt of gratitude. While we embrace the essential skills of asking good questions and listening, we teach a simpler system with the objective of developing your own Line of Investigation to guide you in a dialogue with your clients. If you are getting bogged down with lots of objections your investigation skills of questioning and listening are probably deficient. Remember, without an excellent investigation, there can be no SST.

CHAPTER IV

Four Languages of SST

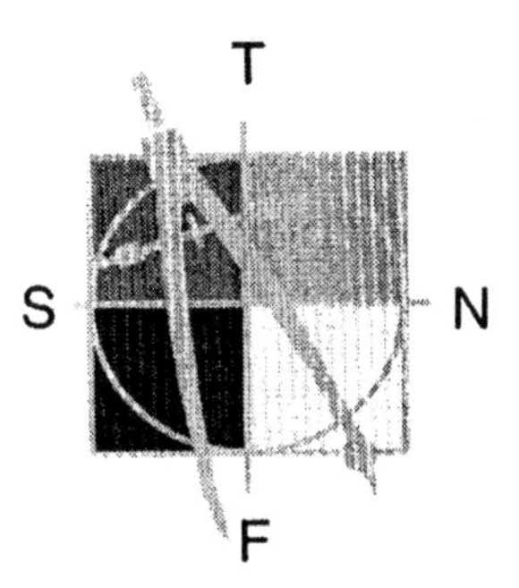

The quadrants of the logo represent the four languages in which we think and communicate. They are determined by combining a natural preference for taking in information (Perceiving) with the second mental function of organizing and acting on the information (Judging).

Taking in Information: S ⟶ N

The Perceiving preferences are Sensing (S) or Intuition (N) and are indicated on the horizontal axis of the logo. Sensors prefer practical, factual and accurate information they can process through their five senses. On the other hand, Intuitives are more interested in what could be than what is, and like to make creative associations and "Intuitive leaps" as they take in information. There are clear implications for selling successfully to type. Sensors like step-by-step presentations loaded with facts describing tried-and-true solutions. Conversely, you risk boring an Intuitive with too many facts. They will be drawn to "big picture" descriptions of cutting edge solutions.

Remember Balance & Shade. In SST, we always need to keep the Balance and Shade rule in front of us. Identifying a Sensing or Intuitive preferred prospect or client does not mean sending messages that are exclusively one or the other. The biggest and easiest value add in learning SST is recognizing our own tendency to emphasize Sensing or Intuition and to be mindful to "Balance" S and N themes in our communication. Even when a prospect's preferences are crystal clear, we don't advocate communication that is all S or N. In these instances, communication should be "Shaded" toward the preference: S or N; or T or F.

Organizing & Deciding:

T

F

The Judging preferences are Thinking (T) and Feeling (F) and are indicated on the vertical axis. Thinking preferred decision makers base decisions on impersonal logical analysis of objectively thought out criteria. If you will, decisions are made with the "head over the heart". Feeling preferred persons, on the other hand, tend to position the "heart over the head" and emphasize values and impact on others in their more subjective decision-making.

Where the Perceiving (Sensing or Intuition) preferences guide us in how we present information, the Judging ones (Thinking or Feeling) orient us to how to most effectively influence decisions. In SST, we persuade Thinkers with logical analyses like cost-benefit or Return on Investment. Forming personal relationships are more important with Feelers as are demonstrating enthusiasm and emphasizing positive personal impact on others. The Balance and Shade rule applies on the Thinking and Feeling dimension as well.

Jungian theory holds that each of us combines a natural preference for taking in information (Sensing or Intuition) with one for organizing and deciding (Thinking or Feeling). Those combinations (ST, SF, NF & NT) indicate our basic way of thinking and communicating.

The outer scales indicate *where* a prospect does his or her best thinking ("Talking it out" for Es and "Thinking it through" for Is) and whether they like matters *settled* (J) or *open* (P). But the heart of SST is in the four languages represented by ST, SF, NF and NT. The ST language is represented in green; SF in red; NF in yellow; and NT in blue.

The practical advantage to this approach is placing the focus on four "kinds of mind" (Lawrence, 1993, p. 189) rather than on sixteen personality types. This makes SST easier to learn. Further it fits the selling process of presenting (S or N) and persuading (T or F).

The remaining chapters will deal with each of the four SST languages. They will begin by describing the common characteristics of ST, SF, NF and NT personalities and then offer a detailed analysis of each of the types.

CHAPTER V

STs: The Stabilizers

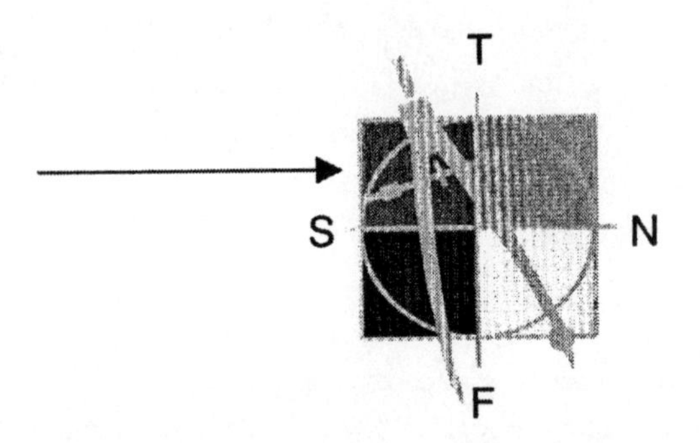

STs, or Stabilizers, prefer to take in information through the "Sensing" function and organize it in a logical fashion using "Thinking". They are drawn to settings where they can work with precise information and evaluate it using objective criteria. Banking, Accounting, the Military and Law Enforcement are popular ST environments. CFOs are typical positions within an organization where it is likely to find Stabilizers.

As their subtitle suggests, they bring stability and objectivity to an organization and will resist getting caught up in unsubstantiated fads or trends. They often focus on conserving resources and will likely want to know about price early on in the dialogue. Generally, they prefer not to clutter their work environment with emotional issues.

When presenting to STs, an orderly step-by-step approach with lots of hard data will be music to their ears. Seek to persuade with logic, citing industry specific illustrations where you can document success.

STs in the Field. We obviously use SST principles when we are selling. One of the predictable behaviors we have seen from STs is their interest in examining all of the sales support materials we have available. For example, if we reinforce our description of SST by referring to a training binder, STs will pick it up and begin to review it. Successful Selling to Type then calls for walking them through the binder describing each module, its activities and outcomes in succession.

This came to life for Harry Koolen when he was making a call with a buying committee of two: an ST and an NT. The NT was the "Economic Buyer" and jumped all around the conversation asking about theory, cutting edge potential and proposing yet a different application. He excused himself from the meeting saying to the ST "User Buyer", "This looks good to me. Let's discuss it later."

The ST buyer then said to Koolen, "There's an awful lot of this that we didn't discuss yet. Bob likes to jump around. Could you take me from the beginning to the end on how this program goes."

Of course, Koolen did. He also won an elephant of a deal

The four ST types are ISTJ, ISTP, ESTP and ESTJ.

ISTJ Buyer Profile

OVERVIEW

ISTJs are found more frequently among men (14% of the time) than among women (8%). They are heavily represented in fields like retail management where, along with their Extraverted counterpart the ESTJ, they comprise roughly 70% of the population. They are also well represented in other occupational fields emphasizing their natural skills with figures such as banking and accounting. ISTJs tend to be both quiet and serious. If only one word could be used to describe the ISTJ, however, it would be dependable. You can count on an ISTJ to get the job done. They have little tolerance for those who don't.

PRELIMINARIES

ISTJs tend to be conservative in everything they do. A fancy, frilly approach will be a turn-off. On the inside of the organization, ISTJs tend to occupy positions with titles like " Controller ". They're the ones raising concerns about the high cost of glossy marketing material. When they're on the receiving end, they have the same reaction. A consistent breed, ISTJs are also conservative dressers. If you're a guy, leave your gold chains at home for this call. Women should dress conservatively as well.

INVESTIGATION

Quiet and serious while they work with the facts and figures, which naturally attract them, ISTJs don't like interruptions. However, as guardians of company resources they will listen to tried and true methods to save money. Similar to approaching their ESTJ counterparts, a long warm-up period for an ISTJ is not only unnecessary, but could even be annoying. They'll want to know the bottom line quickly. It's also important to pace the call with a good sprinkling of questions and probes. Otherwise, potential applications of the product or service you represent could get lost in a race to get to the point.

DEMONSTRATING CAPABILITY

ISTJs will not look to make a change for the sake of changing. If things are working satisfactorily, which to them is getting the task accomplished in an efficient fashion, it's difficult to upset the equilibrium. Novel approaches to solving people problems will hold little appeal to the ISTJ.

Your proposal, both in its written and oral forms, should be chock full of facts. Be certain thet you're accurate in everything you present. A typographical or rounding error would likely go unnoticed by an ENFP, but have been known to sidetrack proposals made to ISTJs. (Just wanted to see if you were reading carefully like a good ISTJ). They always check and double-check their work and expect you to as well.

You don't need to worry about qualifying an ISTJ. Unless your product or service has genuine appeal, and unless they're the appropriate contact in the organization, they'll not waste your time or theirs.

OBTAINING COMMITMENT

Like their Extraverted counterpart the ESTJ, ISTJs tend to be decisive in nature. A proven program which will help them in conserving resources will appeal to the practical and frugal ISTJ. The operative word in the above sentence is *proven.* ISTJs will want "proof" and, in all likelihood, seek to verify what you provide.

ACCOUNT MAINTENANCE

The same "If it's not broke why change it" credo which makes it hard to get in the door to see an ISTJ makes it hard for your competitors once you're in. ISTJs don't require much personal maintenance. That's the good news. The bad news is that if your program or service isn't living up to the agreed upon specifications or terms, it's in jeopardy even if the ISTJ you're dealing with is your sister.

ISTP Buyer Profile

OVERVIEW

A relatively rare type, ISTPs are found in about just 3% of the population. They are best characterized as action oriented realists.

ISTPs are always in pursuit of the most expedient way to get the job accomplished, and like their Extraverted counterparts, the ESTP, frequently behave impulsively. The most common occupational cluster for the ISTP is technical, and while they may be encountered anywhere in the organization, it's more common to find them in support rather than executive roles. For example, positions such as mechanic, dental hygienist, corrections officer and legal secretary are attractive to ISTPs.

PRELIMINARIES

ISTPs are not what you would call social butterflies. As Introspective types, they very much value their private space. Most likely the hottest button you can push for an ISTP will be one that will enable them to do their job more efficiently. Your best bet with an ISTP is appealing to their most immediate needs. If you're selling repairs for their machine which just broke you're far more likely to pique their interest than if you're representing the latest in retirement planning.

INVESTIGATING

This won't be like interviewing the effervescent ESFP. ISTPs tend to go about their business in a detached impersonal fashion. As a rule, ISTPs pursue their hobbies with great vigor. During the initial stages of interviewing the ISTP it's recommended that you seek and probe for information pertaining to recreational interests. ISTPs are the enthusiasts with the fully equipped bass boats and the latest in high tech tennis gear.

As with interviewing all Introspective types, you should anticipate long quiet pauses. ISTPs do their problem solving in their inner worlds.

DEMONSTRATING CAPABILITY

As Sensing types, ISTPs will be drawn to the practical applications of your proposal. They will be relatively disinterested in big picture considerations and equally cool to solutions to people related problems. You should emphasize the logical and short-term benefits of your product or service. Demonstrate how they can complete their jobs more efficiently.

OBTAINING COMMITMENT

If what you represent fixes something that just broke on an ISTP the close can occur pretty quickly. If not, they will need to ponder things in their private space. Being oriented to Perceiving, they are customarily slow to decide preferring to leave things open.

ACCOUNT MAINTENANCE

A well intended unannounced service call might do more harm than good with an ISTP. They will be content if your product or service is meeting its specifications. ISTPs are tricky, however. They're the type of customer who doesn't call to complain or lodge a concern. They will call, however, to cancel the agreement. Keeping informed of how your product or service is performing is crucial but personal contact with the ISTP isn't.

ESTP Buyer Profile

OVERVIEW

ESTPs are action oriented "doers" found in about 3% of the total population. The ESTP is a more common type among men however, being represented 5% of the time compared to 3% for women. Occupational patterns for ESTPs are more difficult to discern than they are for many of the other types. This is because they often enter fields based on the personal relationships they readily establish. Work is more often than not a means to an end for the leisure loving ESTP. Whatever field they're in you'll find them to be outgoing and pragmatic.

PRELIMINARIES

ESTPs are generally friendly folk who are open to sales approaches. They tend to be social and friendly. Given that their work habits are less planned and more spontaneous than they are for types combining Introspection with Judging (ISTJ, INTJ, INFJ & ISFJs), ESTPs are more likely to respond favorably to a drop-in call.

INVESTIGATING

Once engaged in an interview you can expect the ESTP to desire a "get-to-the-point" type of pace. One helpful insight for warming-up, however, is that ESTPs are often involved in sports, as participants, avid fans or both. Again, they take their leisure seriously, and tend to have, or be interested in, state-of-the-art equipment and approaches. As Extraverted types, they frequently decorate their offices with objects of personal importance, often related to their leisure activities.

ESTPs prefer clear and visible explanations. Unlike their Intuitive counterparts, the ENTPs, ESTPs are drawn to hands on kinds of experiences like demonstrations. Expect them to convey their reactions directly and bluntly.

DEMONSTRATING CAPABILITY

With Sensing as their preferred mental function, ESTPs are attracted to proposals that have immediate application. Their orientation tends to be one of, "Let's fix it and get on with it." They have little interest in the theory behind the proposal or long-range possibilities. Therefore, you should lead with concrete evidence that your product or service works and that it will yield results quickly for the ESTP. Like all types combining Sensing for perception with Thinking for decision making (ESTJ, ISTP & ISTJs being the others), ESTPs are bottom line focused.

OBTAINING COMMITMENT

ESTPs are often risk takers who are restless with routine ways of doing business. They're not at all resistant to making changes. If they have an itch and you can scratch it, the sale will close itself. On the other hand, if they conclude that you can't scratch, they'll inform you in a direct fashion. With Thinking as their preferred way of making decisions, ESTPs will weigh your proposal with objective analysis. Given their Extraverted nature, you'll know where they stand.

ACCOUNT MAINTENANCE

If a competitor can show an ESTP that he or she can fix a problem faster or cheaper than you, the account is in jeopardy. Don't allow prolonged stagnancy when serving an ESTP. Demonstrate new developments in your product or service that have direct payoffs. As Extraverted types they'll not mind your dropping in without an appointment. If they can't see you they'll advice you directly and no harm will be done.

ESTJ Buyer Profile

OVERVIEW

ESTJs are excellent organizers and are "Naturals" at business. They value order, procedures and details and are impatient with those who don't. They are a common type in traditional management settings. Taken together, ESTJs and their ISTJ counterparts represent 70% of retail managers. With their skills at "running things", ESTJs frequently rise to top levels of both their work and social organizations. ESTJs are guided by the credo: "If you are what you do, what are you when you don't?" They are the taskmasters of the type table.

PRELIMINARIES

ESTJs are quickly turned-off by sales approaches which appear haphazard and or disorganized. They take their work seriously and expect you to as well. Expect ESTJs to dress appropriately for their role, whatever it may be in the organization. They expect you to also. ESTJs are typically practical and impersonal. Don't expect much time unless the product or service you represent has some direct payoff they can see.

INVESTIGATING

ESTJs are efficient and value their time. They prefer it when sales representatives get to the point. Lengthy warm-up periods are unnecessary for most ESTJs. Expect them to look quickly for bottom line implications. When selling to an ESTJ it's especially important to pace the call with a good balance of questions. Otherwise, potential applications of your product or service may be overlooked in a race to get to the point.

DEMONSTRATING CAPABILITY

ESTJs like it when things are in order and working well. If you encounter an ESTJ in that state it's unlikely that he or she will be interested in making a change. Chances are that they will communicate that to you directly and quickly. Change for the sake of change is not in the common repertoire of the ESTJ. They focus on getting the tasks of their business done efficiently and effectively. Novel ways of solving people problems will have little interest unless a clear bottom line benefit is illustrated. They will be interested in and impressed with past settings where your product or service has improved performance. ESTJs are fluent with numbers and will expect specific and accurate figures to back-up your proposal.

You don't need to worry about wasting time with an ESTJ unqualified to act on a proposal. They follow company protocol carefully and will not meet with you unless they are the appropriate contact.

OBTAINING COMMITMENT

ESTJs are decisive. If the product or service you represent has a concrete payoff for their business they will act quickly. However, there are occasions when ESTJs act too quickly and what appears to be a sale comes undone.

ACCOUNT MAINTENANCE

ESTJs will not require a lot of personal attention. That's the good news. The bad news is that the moment your product or service stops delivering, the account is in jeopardy regardless of whatever kind of personal relationship or relationships you have developed. For this reason, it's important to have a system in place to monitor how your product or service is performing when dealing with ESTJs.

CHAPTER VI

SFs: The Cooperators

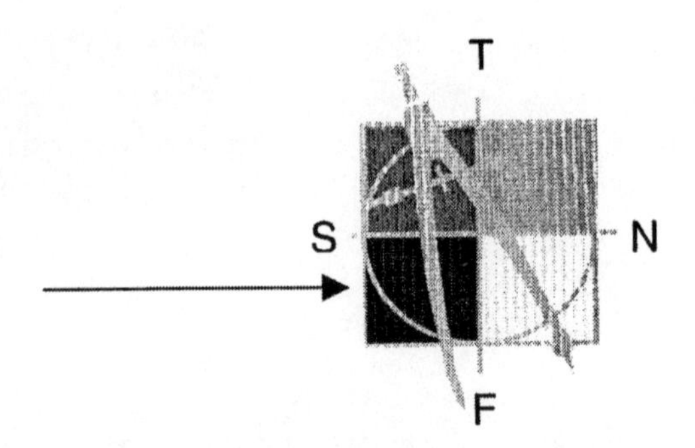

Like the STs, the SF Cooperators prefer Sensing for taking in information and value specific facts and accuracy. However, their preference for evaluating information is Feeling which makes them warmer, more "people oriented" personalities. They are drawn to fields where they can be helpful to others in a hands-on, practical way. Teaching (especially elementary levels) health care and religious work are work settings heavily populated by SFs.

SFs often emphasize "cooperation" at work and seek to promote harmony. They are often gifted at forming warm personal relationships with a wide cadre of co-workers.

Forming and maintaining personal relationships with SF clients and prospects is an effective SST strategy. Taking time getting to know them and learning about their values is time well invested. Presentations should address their Sensing preference and proceed sequentially providing specific facts and details along the way. When seeking to persuade, connect with their values and underscore your solution's positive and practical impact on people.

SFs in the Field. There have been occasions when newly learned SST skills have been successfully applied over a break during training. One notable instance was with an SF Sales Engineer whose key account was on the line. During the SST class he was able to type his client as an NT.

Doug recognized that what he had been doing was sending loud messages in his (Doug's) language and not the client's. He was weighing the NT down with too many facts and seeking to get closer on a personal level. During a break he placed a phone call stressing what he learned were NT themes. "It was like I had been talking in German and his native tongue was French. As soon as I was communicating in his language we started to understand one another. Ultimately, the account was saved and the scope of Doug' assignment with his key account was significantly expanded.

The four SF personalities are: ISFJ, ISFP, ESFP and ESFJ.

ISFJ Buyer Profile

OVERVIEW

ISFJs are found in around 9% of the population and are slightly more common among women than men. Typically quiet and self-effacing, ISFJs are at their best when they are able to help others by providing practical forms of assistance. For example, more ISFJs enter fields like elementary school teaching and nursing than any other type. They're also the most common type found in secretarial positions. When you meet a receptionist, chances are 1 in 4 that he or she is either an ISFJ or ESFJ. ISFJs tend to be sympathetic and kind. They're also meticulously organized and strong with details.

PRELIMINARIES

ISFJs tend to be dedicated workers often working long hours. Their view is that the road to success is more work. As Introspective types, they resent interruptions, which sidetrack them from their work. However, they're rarely rude and will convey warm interest in you and your product or service once you get an appointment. As with all Introspectives, it's advisable to send material for them to review in their private space in advance of the approach.

INVESTIGATING

Like all types with the SJ temperament, ISFJs are content with current arrangements, as long as things are running efficiently. They tend to be cautious about making changes. However, in making their decisions with an emphasis on Feelings and values they will be more interested in solutions to morale problems than their Thinking counterparts, the ISTJ or the ESTJ. The captain of the ISFJ ship is Feeling judgment. However, that process is conducted in the ISFJs private space with Sensing being the able first mate with whom you'll do business during the interview. Therefore, you're well advised to lead with tried-and-true facts regarding how your product or service has worked in other similar settings.

ISFJs follow company policy to the letter. If an ISFJ isn't the right contact, they'll tell you right away. No big qualifying concerns here.

DEMONSTRATING CAPABILITY

Although ISFJs can be found anywhere in the organization's hierarchy, it's more probable that you'll find them as Administrative Assistants who have worked their way up the ladder than as a vice president for marketing recently landed by a headhunter. They have progressed by being good with details and by conserving company resources. Therefore, when making a proposal to an ISFJ it's advisable to provide clear bottom line evidence that your product or service will help conserve resources.

ISFJs tend to be neat freaks. They're the people with carefully organized desks, immaculate cars (including trunks), and closets with everything in its designated place. They value these same characteristics in others. A sloppy presentation will be a major distraction for an ISFJ.

OBTAINING COMMITMENT

ISFJs are meticulous with deadlines as they are with everything else. They rarely put things off. You can expect a clear and timely answer from an ISFJ. The only curve ball will be if you're dealing with an ISFJ office manager who needs to consult with an owner or vice president who's a Perceiving type. This isn't a big fret however, since in this configuration the ISFJ has earned the trust and respect of his or her supervisor. Expect the ISFJ's recommendation to carry the day.

ACCOUNT MAINTENANCE

ISFJs are not a change oriented personality type, and if your product or service is performing up to the agreed upon standards they'll be disinclined to meet with callers representing competing programs or services. This will be especially true if you have paid attention to both the performance of your product or service as well as your personal relationship with the ISFJ.

ISFP Buyer Profile

OVERVIEW

Slightly more common among women than men, ISFPs are found in about 5% of the population. Naturally quiet and self-effacing, some observers describe ISFPs as the most misunderstood type. They rarely share their sentiments in an open and direct way, preferring actions over words. They resemble their Extraverted counterparts, the ESFPs in seeking occupations emphasizing practical ways of helping others such as physical therapy, nursing and counseling. Wherever they are located, ISFPs tend to be to be gentle and caring in their interactions with others.

PRELIMINARIES

Although quiet and reserved, ISFPs tend to be very pleasant people. The word "rude" simply doesn't exist in their vocabularies. As Introspective types, however, they are internally focused and cherish their private spaces. It's always a good idea to schedule an appointment in advance rather than just dropping-by when calling on an ISFP.

INVESTIGATING

Expect ISFPs to be courteous and attentive during the interview. Often, they will be interested in you as well as the product or service you represent. As Perceivers, ISFPs are open to change. ISFPs like to take one step at a time in conversations. If you're an Intuitive type, be careful of your tendency to leap abruptly from one topic to another. Like all Introspective types, ISFPs will be slow to disclose their reactions during the interview.

Given their internal focus and modest nature, there's little need to be concerned about qualifying an ISFP. They'll not volunteer to come out of their private spaces unless they're the appropriate contact point for your call.

DEMONSTRATING CAPABILITY

As Sensors, ISFPs will be drawn to concrete illustrations of your product or service as well as hard evidence that it works. They also tend to be harmonizers who are on the lookout for practical ways of helping others. If possible, you should emphasize facts pertaining to how your product or service has already proven helpful to others. Long-range benefits and theoretical implications will hold considerably less appeal for ISFPs.

OBTAINING COMMITMENT

The closest you can come to egging an ISFP into some form of discourteous behavior is by attempting to force a buy before they have had the opportunity to contemplate a proposal in their private spaces. If your objective is to prompt uncharacteristic behavior, then try to force a close. If, on the other hand, you want to make a sale, give them room. ISFPs are rarely quick to conclude and their decision may take some time. Once you've allowed adequate space and time, be sure to get back to them. They won't object to a follow-up call or two, or even three.

ACCOUNT MAINTENANCE

Given their Introspective orientations, ISFPs are far less fickle than their Extraverted counterparts the ESFPs. They won't be jumping to meet every new representative who comes through the door. Still, being Perceivers, they are open to change and your account is not as secure as it might be with, say an ISFJ. Since they're Feelings oriented decision makers, it's important to pay attention to both personal relationships and product performance when working with ISFPs.

ESFP Buyer Profile

OVERVIEW

Everybody likes an ESFP. They are warm, gregarious and friendly. Slightly more common among women than men, ESFPs represent about 6% of the population. They are generally found in people oriented occupations such as teaching, coaching, social work and respiratory therapy. They are naturally drawn to people and in turn, people are drawn to them. ESFPs bubble with enthusiasm and optimism.

PRELIMINARIES

The good news is that the ESFP approach could be the easiest one in the business. (We'll get to the bad news when we get to "obtaining commitment" below.) ESFPs seek company out and enjoy nothing more than meeting new people. They'll not take your call as an intrusion like the INTP or INTJ. Instead, they will welcome it as an opportunity to meet someone new and, hopefully, interesting. ESFPs have been known to forget appointments, for which they profusely apologize. It's an especially good idea to confirm this one with a cordial, "Looking forward to meeting you" note or with a phone call a few days in advance of the call.

INVESTIGATING

ESFPs, as a rule, are good conversationalists and you will likely enjoy meeting with them as much as they will enjoy meeting you. Expect them to be upbeat and to convey sincere interest, not only in your product or service, but in you as a person. This isn't phony; ESFPs are naturally caring types. You'll find their style to be open and flexible. If what you represent holds appeal to an ESFP they will convey it clearly and directly.

This is a type that requires qualifying, however. Given their natural attraction to people, they may meet with you simply for the sake of meeting someone new.

DEMONSTRATING CAPABILITY

Combining a Sensing, or details orientation to information, with a Feelings oriented decision-making style, ESFPs are particularly attracted to practical solutions to people problems. Unlike the ESTJs, ESFPs tend to be change oriented. Like all Sensing types, they will be struck by hard evidence supporting your proposal.

OBTAINING COMMITMENT

Now for the bad news: ESFPs combine being an easy "Approach" with being one of the toughest "Closes". They are notorious for delaying decision-making. Their ships are captained by the Perceiving mental function of Sensing. This means that they are constantly processing new bits of information. At the risk of injuring feelings, ESFPs will greet the representative following you with the same care and concern shown you. They are the "flirts" of the sales game and, while it's easy to get a date, it's hard to win a long-term commitment.

ACCOUNT MAINTENANCE

Once you get an account with an ESFP, you'll need to work diligently at maintaining it. Attending to your personal relationship with an ESFP can prove as important as monitoring the performance of your product or service. ESFPs are the kind of people who remember everybody's birthday with at least a card, and they will appreciate it if you remember theirs.

ESFJ Buyer Profile

OVERVIEW

The ESFJ personality is one of the types which is more common among women (12%) than men (5%). This disparity is not unusual for types where Feelings are criteria for decision-making. Generally, ESFJs are people who like to help others in a practical way. Occupationally, they meet this need by working as school teachers, nurses and home economists. They're also represented heavily in secretarial and office manager positions. When you meet a receptionist, chances are 1 in 4 that he or she is either ESFJ or ISFJ. ESFJs tend to be well organized and traditional in their values.

PRELIMINARIES

People play a major role in everything the ESFJ does. They generally enjoy meeting new ones. As Extraverted types, they will likely not mind the interruption of a sales call. You can expect them to act personably and tactfully to your approach.

INVESTIGATING

ESFJs are "take charge" types of people who are good at getting things done by organizing other people. With Feelings captaining their ships they do this with care and sensitivity. You'll find that they are tuned into morale issues within the organization and are interested in ideas relating to ways to improve working conditions. Like all types with the SJ combination, however, you'll not find them oriented to change just for the sake of change. During the interview you'll notice that they learn through talking and are more attracted to concrete illustrations than big picture word descriptions. ESFJs typically communicate clearly and quickly where they stand on issues. They like fast paced interviews and your challenge may be to slow the process down with a liberal sprinkling of questions.

ESFJs are careful to follow company protocol and, although they enjoy meeting new people, will be careful to ensure that you're interviewing the right person. If you have any doubts relating to qualifying an ESFJ, just ask and they'll offer a direct and clear answer.

DEMONSTRATING CAPABILITY

Like their Introspective counterpart the ISFJ, it's more likely that you'll be calling on an ESFJ at an office manager level than in the chief executive's suite. Research shows that while ESFJs and ISFJs can be found anywhere in an organization's hierarchy, they represent nearly 25% of office managers compared to just 2 % of CEO's surveyed. It's probable that they climbed the ladder to the office manager position by demonstrating their organizational skills and by following through on assignments. They're "nuts-and-bolts" types and will look for practical solutions and concrete evidence that your proposal works. ESFJs are good with details and will be distracted if you're not. Like their ISFJ counterpart, ESFJs are neat and well organized. Sloppiness in your presentation will be a turn-off.

OBTAINING COMMITMENT

ESFJs are efficient with their time and won't waste yours. They'll want to get to the bottom line quickly. You'll know right where they stand and the cues for the close will be clearly conveyed. The big risk is for an ESFJ to act too quickly and to rule you out without a full appreciation of your proposal. Since they are often office managers or administrative assistants, ESFJs may need to get clearance for a new initiative. The final approval may take a little longer in this scenario, but ultimately the ESFJs recommendation will be followed.

ACCOUNT MAINTENANCE

Personal relationships are important to ESFJs and it will be important to monitor not only the performance of your product or service but to attend to your relationship with the ESFJ as well. This is especially significant early on when the ESFJ may have second thoughts about a decision. Remember, unlike their ISFJ counterparts, the Extraverted ESFJ will be quick to act. Once established with an ESFJ, it's likely that you'll have a secure account as long as your product or service is delivering.

CHAPTER VII

NFs: The Catalysts

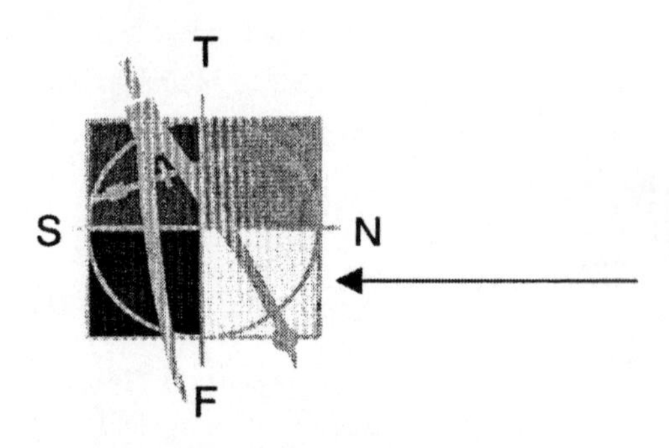

NFs or Catalysts are drawn to the "big picture" and possibilities through their perceiving preference of Intuition. Often they have a long term and global perspective on matters. With their Feeling preference for organizing and acting on information, they typically emphasize broad human values. They are quite idealistic in their approach to work and life in general. NFs typically have a well-developed artistic appreciation.

While STs characteristically resist change, NFs are typically "Catalysts" to doing things differently. This is particularly true if change will make the organization more responsive to individual development. They are attracted to fields like Counseling, Human Resources, Behavioral Sciences and the arts.

When presenting to NFs appeal to their natural interest in doing things differently. Lead with "big picture" and long-range considerations. Be prepared to accommodate "Intuitive Leaps" they may take. Don't for example, say, "That is in slide 26 and we are only on slide four." Just as with the SFs, building personal relationships and connecting with their values is effective SST strategy with NFs.

<u>NFs in the Field</u>. As noted above, NFs are frequently drawn to the Human Resources field. There they relate with people and their development (F) at the policy and program development level (N). In his mix of consulting services that includes SST, Russ Brooks represents and oversees the delivery of a franchised time management system. He frequently encounters NF buyers in the Human Resources department and, applying SST, has crafted his delivery of the time management value proposition. Russ offers this account:

"With the "Thinking" preferred CEOs I relate with I underscore and document productivity gains using our system. However, when I address NF prospects, I emphasize work-life balance issues and how the system actually creates time for personal development, leisure and family. Recently, I had an experience where an NF in Human Resources actually changed her body posture when I highlighted those themes. She sat up and moved closer. It was clear that she was attending to my messages in a focused fashion. We won a nice deal. This is not an isolated experience. In fact it has been replicated many times."

Then of course, there is the classic illustration of the Information Technology sales team who arrived for their meeting with a prospect a few minutes late. There was an array of reasons for their tardiness; not the least of which was a wayward technician who had to be rounded up. Feeling somewhat apprehensive when they got to the client, who the sales member of the team had typed as an NF before the meeting, they were immediately put at ease. The client "apologized" for her shabby directions and what must have been a stressful trip. "We know that's not the response we would have received from a "T" buyer." They are right.

INFJ Buyer Profile

OVERVIEW

Found in around 5% of the population, INFJs are slightly more common among women than men. INFJs can be described as quiet idealists and although they succeed in many different occupational settings, it's more typical to find them in roles where they are assisting others such as teaching, library work, social work and the clergy. Often there's a distinctive intellectual bent with INFJs, not unlike their "Thinking" counterparts the INTJs. For example, they are among the top three types represented in the prestigious college scholastic honorary, Phi Beta Kappa. Although they are champions of lofty ideals, they rarely advertise that fact. The saying, "Still water runs deep" aptly describes many INFJs.

PRELIMINARIES

Like many Introspective types, INFJs can be difficult to read. This is because they exercise their favored mental function, decision making from a "Feelings" perspective, in their preferred private worlds. Although they are extremely sensitive to others, they often appear quiet and reserved. Those who naively believe that "people oriented people" are loud and active will often misread INFJs.

Like the approach to all Introspective types, scheduling an appointment and sending materials in advance are recommended for an INFJ. They tend to be talented with the written word and will appreciate well-crafted marketing material, which incidentally, is another area where INFJs excel.

INVESTIGATING

Caring-yet-reserved is the best way to describe the INFJ on the other end of your interview. They will listen attentively, usually with the uncanny empathy which characterizes the INFJ. Like other Introspective types, you should expect them to be cautious in disclosing their reactions to what you discuss. While they're slow to reveal their values, you can bet they are deeply held. INFJs like to buy from people they like; people who are informed, caring and sensitive. Probably the worst thing you could do when interviewing an INFJ would be to light up a cigarette while recounting an ethnic joke.

DEMONSTRATING CAPABILITY

The INFJs of the world are intrigued by "big" ideas which will have a positive impact on the human condition. Like others preferring Intuition for their Perceiving function, INFJs will be far more intrigued by the long range implications and possibilities of your proposal than by the details which support it. Some refer to the INFJs as the "Poets of the Type Table". They value skilled language expression, particularly if it is enhanced with the creative use of imagery. This doesn't mean that you need to write or speak in iambic pentameter to win the sale; only that if you're able to work in some nice imagery in the proposal it won't go unnoticed by an INFJ.

OBTAINING COMMITMENT

When INFJs say, "I'll think it over and get back to you"; they're not brushing you off. They mean it. Those of us who do our decision-making in our private worlds (Introspective Judgers and Extraverted Perceivers) need privacy and solitude to make a decision. This isn't the kind of a close you should expect to make in the INFJs office. INFJs are decisive, however, and once given the room they need to ruminate you can expect them to act quickly.

ACCOUNT MAINTENANCE

Servicing an account where you're relating to an INFJ can be tricky. While they value personal relationships they're hardly "Hail, fellow! Well met." kinds of people. Like other Introspective "Feelers" (INFP, ISFP, and INFJs), INFJs value personal relationships. Just don't barge into their offices in search of them. They'll appreciate it if you check on their satisfaction with the product or service you represent with an appointment.

INFP Buyer Profile

OVERVIEW

INFPs are the idealists of the type table. Quiet and intelligent, they are often committed to lofty causes; the kind which will make the world a better place. Those who guess the type of historical figures suggest that Joan of Arc was an INFP. About as common among men as among women, INFPs represent about 7% of the population. However, they are the most common type among both Phi Beta Kappa's and Rhodes Scholars (13% and 21% respectively). INFPs are most heavily represented in helping occupations such as counselor or social worker, or those with an artistic bent such as writer.

PRELIMINARIES

While their Extraverted counterpart, the ENFP, is likely the most approachable personality type, the INFP is much trickier. INFPs often strike others as reserved, or even shy. However, once the superficial is out of the way, INFPs can be very engaging types demonstrating an uncommon depth of feeling combined with a quick wit and a disarming sense of humor. Initial encounters may feel cool but will likely warm-up. Like all NP types (ENFP, ENTP and INTP), the INFP is typically attracted to big picture considerations rather than the details related to it. As Perceivers, they welcome new ideas, but since their source of energy is internal, they resent interruptions. Providing written material in advance is a good strategy for approaching the INFP. Chances are they will read it.

INVESTIGATING

As Introspective types, INFPs use their favorite mental function, for them Intuition, in their private space. They will be racing off with ideas and seeing possibilities during the interview but will only disclose some of them with you. Don't be tricked into hammering away at features and benefits you think the INFP has missed. They haven't. Pace the interview with liberal questioning and allow the INFP ample quiet time for concentration. INFPs are comfortable with quiet even if Extraverted sellers are not. It's less important to qualify the INFP than it is for their Extraverted sisters and brothers, the ENFP.

DEMONSTRATING CAPABILITY

INFPs will be especially attracted to proposals that will improve the human condition. The more global and the more humane the proposal the better it is. For example, a proposal that will help improve the quality of life for workers will be far more attractive than one that will reduce the unit cost of widgets, but at the expense of working conditions. They're not as change oriented as those Perceiving types who are Intuitive and Extraverted (ENFP and ENTP). However, they are far less resistant to change, particularly when it will improve morale, than those types combining Sensing and Judging (ESTJ and ISTJ).

OBTAINING COMMITMENT

INFPs could be the toughest "close" in the business. In their pursuit of perfection and idealistic goals, they are notoriously deliberate in making decisions. With Intuition as their favorite mental function, they are always open to yet *one more possibility.* Along with the ISFP, they are the slowest to make decisions relative to college majors and careers, for example. Getting an INFP to act will likely require multiple, but gentle, nudges. Always emphasize the big picture as well as positive impact on people and organizational values.

ACCOUNT MAINTENANCE

With Feelings as their favored criteria for decision-making, personal relationships are important to the INFP. It's better to make arrangements to see them in advance rather than just dropping in, however. As Introspective types they like to work with their doors closed and dislike interruptions. Your agenda for this service call should focus on how your product or service has had an impact on morale and or organizational mission.

ENFP Buyer Profile

OVERVIEW

ENFPs are popular, even charismatic people. With their uncanny skills at understanding and empathizing with others, they exert an impact on society well beyond what would be predicted by their 5% representation in the population. They are typically zestful and enthusiastic people who are heavily represented in "helping" fields like counseling and social work. ENFPs tend to be creative and it is not uncommon for them to have artistic talent. Almost all have a clear appreciation for the arts.

PRELIMINARIES

ENFPs may be the easiest personality type to approach. They are warm, cordial and friendly. As a rule, they enjoy meeting new people, especially those offering new ideas. Unlike an ISTJ, for example, ENFPs would far prefer talking with a sales representative than catching up on paper work. About the latter, ENFPs are notorious for having many projects underway at once and their workstations tend to look disorganized. ENFPs enjoy a good joke or story, as long as it's not the variety that demeans others.

INVESTIGATING

As Extraverted types they learn through talking and will review out-loud many potential applications for your product or service, perhaps some you haven't even entertained. Don't be fooled into thinking that they are committing, however. They're merely thinking out-loud. You'll probably feel that you have established a personal relationship with an ENFP within a short period of time. Most people do. In dealing with ENFPs, qualifying is important because you may spend time, albeit in engaging conversation, which won't lead ultimately to a sale.

DEMONSTRATING CAPABILITY

ENFPs are always on the lookout for novel ways of doing things. They are particularly tuned into personnel issues and anxious to improve working conditions. With Intuition as their dominant mental function they are quick to see the big picture. They will be less concerned with facts, at least initially.

OBTAINING COMMITMENT

Although naturally intrigued by new ideas, their Perceiving orientation leaves ENFPs constantly open to new ones. The moment you leave their office they may be equally enticed by yet another new idea. This tendency coupled with their need to maintain harmony within the organization through participatory decision-making tends to make ENFPs slow decision makers. While they maybe the easiest type to get to see, the bad news is that they are among the slowest in acting on a proposal.

ACCOUNT MAINTENANCE

ENFPs will value their business relationship with you. Niceties such as birthday cards, Christmas gifts etc. will be appreciated as will regular stops to service the account. In this instance, "servicing" applies to both the performance of your product or service and the personal relationships you have established.

ENFJ Buyer Profile

OVERVIEW

ENFJs tend to be socially adept people who are very popular with their peers. As is the case with most types preferring Feelings for decision-making, ENFJs are slightly more common among women than men. While they are represented overall in roughly 6% of the population, it is far more common to find them in occupational settings emphasizing their priority of being of service to others: counseling, teaching, social work, and religious work. ENFJs tend to have a creative flair and they are often active in the arts. This creative thread can generally be detected, however, in whatever they do.

PRELIMINARIES

Warm and gracious by nature, ENFJs are usually an easy approach. Combining Intuition as their Perceiving function with a Feelings orientation to decision making, ENFJs will be particularly attracted to creative solutions to people problems or issues. They combine their caring attitude with precise organization and it's typically unnecessary to remind them of the appointment.

INVESTIGATING

As Extraverts, ENFJs learn best through talking. You'll find ENFJs to be both personable and highly skilled verbally. ENFJs are skilled listeners and they will track you closely as you speak, often offering non-verbal support such as head nodding. They value good listening skills and you are well advised to display them as well. You'll quickly learn where you stand when interviewing an ENFJ.

Unlike their perceiving counterparts, the ENFPs, ENFJs carefully manage their time and rarely over-commit to too many projects. They are like the ENFP, however, in displaying a keen wit and a good sense of humor. Neither appreciate jokes at someone else's expense. While they enjoy meeting people, as most Extraverts do, there's little qualifying concern with an ENFJ. This is due to their Judging orientation to conducting business and their careful time management. They wouldn't waste yours or theirs.

DEMONSTRATING CAPABILITY

ENFJs will be fast to recognize the big picture implications of your product or service and will be less attracted to the details and facts that support it. ENFJs like finding creative solutions to problems, particularly those affecting people. This is what you should feature in the proposal.

OBTAINING COMMITMENT

ENFJs tend to be both direct communicators and well organized. The requisite steps to get to a commitment should be clearly evident when dealing with an ENFJ. They are frequently leaders who employ a participatory decision making style. In this configuration decisions are slower to evolve, but the ENFJ will readily layout the expected time frame for you.

ACCOUNT MAINTENANCE

With an ENFJ it's important to monitor both the performance of your product or service and to pay attention to your personal relationship. Regarding the latter, ENFJs prefer appointments and service calls which focus on novel approaches to developing the talents of people in the organization or exploring other ways of serving people.

CHAPTER VIII

NTs: The Visionaries

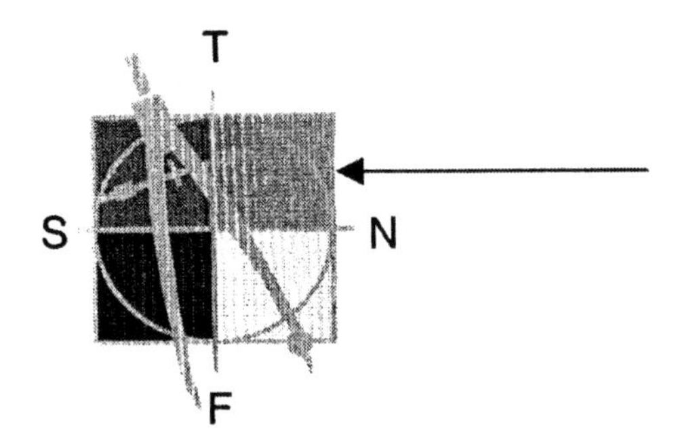

NTs, or Visionaries, prefer to use Intuition for taking in information. Like NFs they are drawn to the "big picture" and possibilities. They would rather stand back to get a long-range perspective on the "forest", than study the specifics of all of the "trees". Like the STs they prefer to emphasize impersonal logic in their decision-making. Typical fields attractive to NTs include Law, Higher Education, Architecture and Computer Science.

The combination of long-range perspective with objective analysis positions NTs for a disproportionate number of executive assignments. That is to say, NTs are simultaneously the rarest group in the general population while being the most common type among executives.

In proposing to NTs, it is good SST strategy to emphasize the competitive advantage your solution will deliver. Keep your facts concise and be prepared for a wide-ranging dialogue focusing on future and innovative applications. Persuade with logical analysis emphasizing Return on Investment considerations.

NTs in the Field. Our prospect was the VP for Sales and Marketing in an industry where he knew he had a distinctive product, but his team was consistently falling short of its targets. He isolated the issues down to selling skills and not product differentiation. Committed to improving performance, he first arranged for a former IBM sales trainer to deliver programs to improve selling skills. It was a disaster. Not only was the training expensive, but it made no difference in performance.

Intuitively, the VP determined that the issue still had to do with sales skills. But, he believed that initial trainer with the IBM background taught the wrong skills. With healthy skepticism as a guide, he launched a search for sales education that would be the right key to his firm's lock.

SST was included in their search. In our first meeting he was quickly intrigued by the application of Jung's theory to selling. In fact, he had previously been introduced to Jung through an MBTI based management development program. But, regardless of how interesting the SST program sounded, this time he wanted hard proof that it would work.

This is one of the many instances where prospects "scream" their SST preferences. Our prospect was very much drawn to the theory behind SST and clearly in search of cutting edge solutions. These are clearly N or Intuitive characteristics. His Thinking preference was demonstrated by desiring the hard evidence that SST would improve performance and that investment in training would have a justifiable business return.

We proposed a classic Experimental and Control Group study for a business quarter. At the end of that period, we would compare the performance of the Experimental Group trained in SST against that of the remaining sales staff constituting the Control Group.

When the results were in we were delighted to discover that the Experimental Group with SST outperformed the Control Group by 488%. Obviously, we were engaged to train the rest of the sales force.

The four NT personalities are: INTJ, INTP, ENTP and ENTJ.

INTJ Buyer Profile

OVERVIEW

Found only in about 1% of the population, INTJs are the most self-confident personality found in the "SST Human Grid". They are also the most independent, enjoying doing things differently than others. While they are open to new concepts, they are both analytical and practical in their evaluation. Rank or title of the presenter mean little to the INTJ; catchy slogans even less. Presenters must be competent and any proposal needs to pass the rigors of the private scrutiny of the INTJ. Populating executive suites, law offices, laboratories, architectural firms, or found on college faculties, INTJs will construct systems approaches to their business given the slightest opportunity. INTJs are often the initiators and promoters of ideas.

PRELIMINARIES

Approaching an INTJ can be tricky. While they are naturally intrigued by new ideas and solutions, they hate to be interrupted if they're involved in a meaningful project. Don't expect that a gimmick will get you in the door. But, if you have confidence in your product or service, and if you're competent in selling it, definitely knock. Many INTJs like written material in advance of the call. Literature focusing on future possibilities with both a cover letter and business card can work well. Be prepared to offer more than one of the latter, business cards that is, because INTJs are notoriously bad with names.

INVESTIGATING

INTJs are adept learners and will need little assistance in seeing the big picture. Be consultative and questioning allowing the INTJ to determine the length of the discovery stage. If it takes more than one meeting, that's a good sign. INTJs don't waste time on matters unimportant to them. Expect them to be direct and businesslike. Don't be surprised if they ask for more material or references they can track down. It will be impressive if you can produce back-up material or a list of references upon request. Good preparation is a way to display competence. INTJs like to study an idea in their private space.

DEMONSTRATING CAPABILITY

When it's time to make the proposal, do so directly and competently. INTJs are usually in higher levels of the organization and if they spend the time with you they are qualified to act on you proposal. INTJs will balance their natural attraction to the possibilities and novel applications to new situations with a rigorous pragmatism. The possibilities of your proposal are what will sell; but a failure to offer competent responses to pragmatic concerns can kill it. Rarely will an INTJ give away his or her reaction to your proposal. If they like it, they'll want to study it privately before acting. INTJs will never allow themselves to commit to a trial close unless they intend to commit.

OBTAINING COMMITMENT

Allow them to pace the closing of the sale. This will not be time wasted. INTJs don't waste their time nor will they waste yours. Decisions will be made on merit and not on personal relationship. There's no reason to fear asking for the order because INTJs expect it and recognize it as part of your job. INTJs trust their ability to make good decisions.

ACCOUNT MAINTENANCE

Once decided, you should have a long-term customer in an INTJ. Like their sensing counterparts, the ISTJ, INTJs require little in the way of personal attention. In fact, just "dropping-by" would be an intrusion. Criteria for maintaining the account will hinge on performance. If the product or service you represent doesn't perform up to the agreed upon standards, INTJs will make changes, your considerable personable charm notwithstanding.

INTP Buyer Profile

OVERVIEW

A relatively uncommon type overall, INTPs are highly represented in settings recognizing academic achievement. While they show-up just 4% of the time in the general population, they are the most frequent recipients of National Merit Scholarships. They're Judging brothers and sisters, the INTJs, are a close second. Typically quiet and reserved, INTPs are logical thinkers with a powerful ability to concentrate. They're at home in their private space dealing with ideas. Generally low-key people, INTPs become aggressive if a principle they value is violated.

PRELIMINARIES

INTPs cherish quiet. A cold call representing a familiar product or service will likely strike an INTP as an intrusion. They are attracted to ideas however, and if you represent a product or service which appeals to their intellectual bent you should definitely call. With a Perceiving orientation, INTPs enjoy the intellectual challenges associated with meaningful change. One INTP college faculty member was known to drive his departmental colleagues crazy with his desire to change the curriculum every year or two.

As with the approach to all Introspective types, you should definitely send material they can review in their inner world before you call. Like the other types with the NT combination or temperament (INTJ, ENTP, and ENTJ'S being the others) they place a high value on competence. To get the attention of an INTP the earlier you display competency, the better off you will be.

INVESTIGATING

Others often describe INTPs as being "lost in thought". They're not lost at all. They're simply doing the rigorous intellectual analysis they value and do well in their private worlds. Allow them space and time to do their thinking. Chatter without purpose will strike them as aimless and annoying. Expect long quiet pauses while they ponder.

INTPs are fast learners and need little help seeing implications and possibilities of your product or service. As NTs they're good at finding flaws, but unlike the Extraverted NT's, the ENTJ and the ENTP, INTPs will be less likely to point hem out. (That typo is probably safe.) Here they resemble the INTJ. If you get an interview with an INTP there's little need to qualify. They wouldn't come out of their intellectual tents unless they wanted to meet with you. Don't take that personally. This call hinges on the merits of your product or service and has much less to do with your personal charm, albeit considerable.

DEMONSTRATING CAPABILITY

Intuitive in nature, INTPs will be quickly drawn to the big picture implications of your proposal. Proposals that are cutting edge will hold far more appeal than those addressing people oriented issues. INTPs are known for wanting the precise meaning of words you use in your proposal. As a rule, they prefer tight grammatically correct language. With a Thinking orientation to decision making, they will objectively consider data and evidence supporting a proposal.

OBTAINING COMMITMENT

Like their Extraverted counterpart, the ENTP, the INTP personality is typically risk taking in character. They are attracted to big picture considerations and are generally bored by day-to-day operational details. Although they are change advocates themselves, they typically need to consult with others in the organization since the scope of change they entertain is major. While they recognize the importance of saving pennies on the margin, they would prefer for someone else to attend to those matters while they contemplate revolutionary ways of conducting business. Since executing revolutionary ideas involves many in the organization, they need to consult with others. This takes time and can draw out the closing process when dealing with an INTP.

ACCOUNT MAINTENANCE

Maintaining an account with an INTP will be determined solely on the merits of your product or service. Keep in touch with the INTP to be informed of performance and related concerns. Respect the sanctity of the INTPs private space, however. Idle chatter will have the same effect on the INTP as running your fingernail across a blackboard.

ENTP Buyer Profile

OVERVIEW

ENTPs are among the most competitive of the sixteen personality types. They thrive on their ability to find clever, even ingenious solutions to problems. They love to be "one-up" whether it's with a social golf opponent or with an important business competitor.

Like their ENFP counterparts, they are interested in, and usually well informed, on a wide array of topics. As a rule, they are well read and are good conversationalists. ENTPs typically have an enterprising spirit which, combined with their independent nature, frequently leads them into entrepreneurial ventures.

PRELIMINARIES

Where ENFPs welcome almost all sales approaches, the ENTP is more fickle. As Thinking decision makers they are less concerned with feelings than the ENFP, but just as intrigued by new ideas and the novel approach for which they are in constant quest. If you represent a product or service that is cutting-edge, or at least new to them, they will anxiously and graciously meet with you. However, if you represent something they've already considered and rejected, getting an interview with an ENTP can be more challenging than getting tickets to the NCAA FINAL FOUR.

INVESTIGATING

ENTPs have a knack for seeing relations others miss. They are generally quick learners who learn best through the give-and-take of a good conversation, including the one you can engineer with your sales call. Like their other NT counterparts (INTJ, INTP, and the ENTJ) they value competence in sales representatives. If you don't display it in the first interview it's unlikely that you'll have a second chance. Careful qualifying is usually unnecessary when calling on an ENTP, unless they are curious in what you represent and then they may meet with you simply to learn more about it. ENTPs are relentless in their pursuit of new ideas.

DEMONSTRATING CAPABILITY

With Intuition as their dominant mental function, ENTPs are more drawn to the big picture and less interested in the facts that support it. They are change oriented like the ENFP but, unlike that type, more attracted to systems solutions and getting a competitive edge than finding ways to solve "people problems".

OBTAINING COMMITMENT

Characteristically, ENTPs are risk takers. For major decisions they apply the logic of their Thinking preference for making decisions and will act only after a rigorous analysis. Given their attraction to the big picture and their general lack of interest in details, they may consult with someone who's attracted to numbers before they act. This approach is especially common if the person or persons with whom the ENTP consults reinforces his or her "learn through talking" style. For more minor decisions, ENTPs have been known to "bungee jump" pretty quickly, particularly if they feel they're not boxed into a long-term contract.

ACCOUNT MAINTENANCE

The effectiveness of your product or service is the ultimate criterion for the ENTP. If it's doing what he or she hoped, the account is secure; if it's not the ENTP will be quick to make a change. Service calls are important, but be prepared to discuss new developments in the field rather than manufacturing small talk.

ENTJ Buyer Profile

OVERVIEW

Found in about 5 % of the population, ENTJs are take charge leaders. This is true from elementary school right through to senior years in corporations, law firms or universities. ENTJs are not shy about seeking prestige and the money which accompanies it. They get ahead through hard work and making tough decisions along the way. ENTJs have been known to become their jobs.

PRELIMINARIES

As Extraverted types, ENTJs are generally open to sales approaches which are professional and will enable them to solve problems. Although they behave much like their Sensing counterpart the ESTJ, ENTJs will be more attracted to broad policy solutions. ENTJs are natural strategic thinkers and often relate to the strategic planning function in an organization. Therefore, approaches relating to the highest level concerns, or mission, of the organization will hold the greatest appeal to an ENTJ. In fact, it's a good idea to review the organization's mission statement to help you plan your approach.

INVESTIGATING

As Extraverted Thinkers, you'll find ENTJs to be straightforward and direct during the interview. They learn best by talking. Like all types with the NT combination (INTJs, INTPs, and ENTPs being the others), ENTJs place a high value on competence and professionalism. They will display both during the interview and will expect you to as well. ENTJs are oriented to the big picture and enjoy conversations that are global and broad based in character. Be prepared to back-up any sweeping generalizations you may be inclined to make with facts. " Where are your data? ", is a common question posed by ENTJs.

ENTJs are ambitious and typically rise to higher levels of their organization. They're also very competitive. Qualifying an ENTJ often depends on age. A rising star may want to meet with someone representing a novel solution to learn all he or she can <u>without</u> the authority to buy. This is less likely to be a problem with an established star.

DEMONSTRATING CAPABILITIY

Gaining a competitive advantage always appeals to the ENTJ, and that's what you want to stress in your proposal. Although drawn to the big picture by their Intuitive preference for attending to information, the ENTJ, like her Introspective sister the INTJ, will lead with Thinking and the objective analysis which characterizes that mental function. Have your facts well organized and straight when offering your proposal to an ENTJ.

As suggested above, ENTJs are strategic thinkers who will be attracted to proposals which can enable the organization to accomplish its strategic goals. They also abhor inefficiency and will be intrigued by proposed solutions to help their operations run more efficiently.

OBTAINING COMMITMENT

By nature, ENTJs are decisive and action oriented. The settlement of this call will be determined on the merits of your product or service and will close itself. This doesn't suggest a quick close, however. ENTJs learn by talking to others and will likely want to bounce your proposal off one or two others they respect prior to deciding.

ACCOUNT MAINTENANCE

ENTJs are objective and accustomed to making tough decisions. If your product or service isn't delivering in the agreed upon fashion it will be as easy for an ENTJ to make a change as it is to order lunch. (Typically, ENTJs know what they want without looking at a menu.) For this account the criteria for continuation relate exclusively to product performance and not to personal relationships.

Chapter IX

Four Buyer Influences

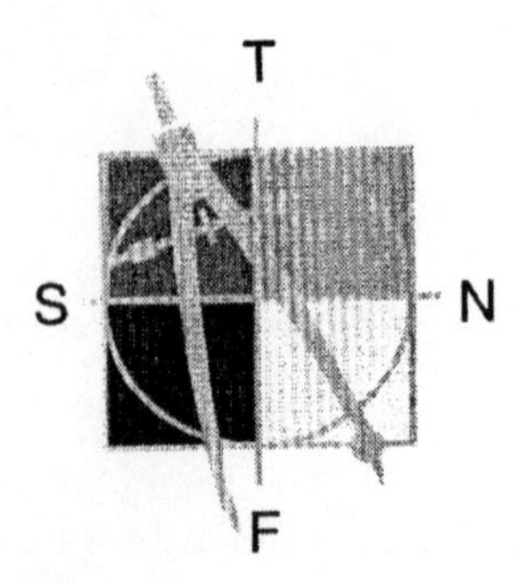

Not long ago a participant in SST approached me during a break and observed:

"I am a student of consultative selling and I have always thought that if someone could fuse Rackham's SPIN with Miller and Heiman's Buyer Influences they would have a great model. You have done that and added a powerful new piece for me: personality types."

It was one of those occasions when you wish you had a tape recorder to play the conversation back. Obviously, it holds marketing implications. But if you will allow, it was even more rewarding because this person truly understood what SST is all about. It was music to my ears because he also understood me.

Throughout the course of this book I have contrasted SST to "old school selling". This is the approach captured by manipulative techniques and characterized by a few fairly hideous bromides like:

- The sale doesn't start until the prospect says "No"
- Close them early and often

- ABC: Always Be Closing
- Selling requires testosterone (The civilized interpretation)

The underling premise is that prospects and clients are adversaries and a really clever closing technique, or an artful handling of an objection, were the keys to winning a sale. Clearly, those views and techniques are very foreign to our approach with SST.

There are, however, two other consultative selling models we embrace that are wholly compatible with SST. One is Neil Rackham's SPIN that heavily influences our approach to the investigation and is described in Chapter Three. The second referenced by our flattering student is "Four Buyer Influences" (Miller & Heiman, 1985 & 1998).

The buyer influences model is straightforward and simple to master. If you are not already familiar with it, it can add a great deal to your selling success. Basically, the investigation and then communicating to type are skills that are applied to, not just a single buyer, but to "Four Buyer Influences".

If we were to illustrate the SST process as influenced by Rackham and Miller & Heiman it would look like this:

Buyer Influences			
Economic	User	Technical	Advocate
Investigate	Investigate	Investigate	Investigate
Balance	Balance	Balance	Balance
Shade	Shade	Shade	Shade

Balance & Shade. Now, if you are one of those Intuitive readers like me, you may have jumped to this chapter without reading the explanations of "Balance" and "Shade" (Chapter One) in preceding ones. "Balance" fundamentally means ensuring that your messages appeal to all four communication styles and not just your own. To "Balance" all you need to know in terms of type methodology is your own personality and your tendency to send communication the way you would like to receive it. "Shade" comes into play when we have sufficient time with prospects and clients to confidently read their preferences. When we know style preferences we "Shade" our communication toward them. When we are unsure, we take care to balance our messages.

Four Buyer Influences

One of the major differentiators between commodity, or transactional, selling and the consultative selling is the presence of multiple buying influences at the consultative level. When selling at the commodity level the seller typically seeks to influence one buyer that his or her product is the best value and that it is easy to acquire. Small transaction selling emphasizes working hard and getting in front of as many qualified decision makers as possible. It's knock on the door, make the pitch, try for the close and move on to the next door as quickly as possible.

At the consultative level, however, there are multiple buying influences at play. While working hard never hurt, it is not enough unless accompanied by smart strategies for various buyer influences. Miller and Heiman's Strategic Selling (1985) and New Strategic Selling (1998) made a major contribution in understanding multiple buyer influences.

In major and complex sales, there are four influences that you need to manage: Economic; User; Technical and Advocate or Coach. Before we define each one of the influences, it is important to emphasize that these are "roles" that can be played by the same person. If we were playing a zone defense strategy for a basketball game, there would be defensive assignments for opposing offensive players moving into the different zones in the defense. If a player leaves the game it is not as though we can relax and ignore his or her substitute. Similarly, we need to have constant and continuing focus for all four influences and recognize that, just as in basketball, the same player can shoot, pass and rebound on different plays.

Economic Buyer

As the title suggests, this is the person who controls the purse strings for the decision. In the transactional model, the focus is exclusively on the Economic Buyer and the purpose of qualifying is to identify him or her. In major and complex sales, however, the economic buyer consults with others to get "buy in" on the decision. Economic Buyers have the following characteristics:

- Can give final approval
- Control dollars
- Have veto power
- Bottom line focus
- Asks, "What are we going to see as ROI?"

User Buyers

Where the Economic Buyer is typically a single person, Users as a rule are several or many. They are the people who will be using your product on a regular basis. Sometimes, the Economic Buyer will seek to gain buy-in by consulting with a representative User or a committee comprised of them.

From the Field. We worked with a client a few years ago who sold employee health benefits. Prior to applying the multiple buyers model their representatives would call exclusively on Economic Buyers; in this instance the highest-ranking HR person they could reach.

The HR person would typically advise our client's rep that they intended to take their information to get reactions from others inside the organization. From there, End Users would raise questions that the HR person couldn't, or didn't want to answer. Eventually, the HR person would ask themselves, "Why am I spending all this time selling their product?" Their answer was that they shouldn't be.

A major break trough occurred when, at out urging, our client's reps began to take the initiative in meeting with representative or a committee of Users. Questions were answered and confidence gained. Often, the Users would come back to the Economic Buyer asking to try our client's product.

User Buyers have the following characteristics:

- They will be the one's using your product
- There will be several or many
- They will assess the impact of your product on their jobs or lives
- How will this product work for me?

Technical Advisers

These are the invisible influences that can undo a deal you thought you had won. By definition they are the technical experts to whom the Economic Buyer will turn to ensure that whatever you are proposing fits all the tech specs and protocols already in place. Unlike the User influence, the Technical Adviser can be a single person.

From the Field. Our client had what they considered world-class software, heretofore marketed exclusively to the military. Instead of the automatic wins they anticipated when they rolled it out commercially, they suffered a series of losses to competitors they were certain had inferior products.

Accustomed to a military sale where the highest in command called the shot and drove it down the organization, our client found private financial buyers were consulting with both Users and Technical Advisers. Feeling left out of the loop, the Technical Advisers, would say, "No, their (our client's) program is technically incompatible with what we do now." End of deal.

Technical Advisers have the following characteristics:

- Screen out proposals
- Can't say "yes" but can say "no"
- Focus on technical specifications
- Often wear pocket protectors

Advocate or Coach

By now you might be asking yourself, "How do I figure out who the players are when my prospect doesn't provide score cards?" The answer is that your "Advocate" can provide this vital information.

The Advocate is someone who has insights about who will be influencing the decision for which you are contending. Often, but not always, they are inside the organization. They do, however, always have these attributes in common:

- They want to see you win
- You have credibility with them
- They can provide and interpret "insider" information.
- They will work with you

Wins, Results & SST

Miller & Heiman introduced the four-buyer influences model in 1985 in Strategic Selling. Thirteen years later, they authored The New Strategic Selling.

Like others, you may be asking, "So what is new?"

In the new version, the authors stress the importance of understanding clients as people and not just businesses. They use the terms "Win and Results" to make this point.

Results are corporate and pertain to business gains your product provides. They are usually measured objectively and include:

- Increased profit
- More sales
- Growth
- Productivity increased
- Costs cut
- Quality improved
- Trouble avoided e.g. Law suits
- Image improved
- Company saved

Wins are personal and more subjective than business results. They include:

- Career advancement
- Resume builder
- Incentive pay
- Recognition from superiors
- Recognition within the industry
- Job(s) saved
- Company saved
- Personal expression
- Sense of accomplishment

"It's never enough to sell results alone." (Heiman and others, 1998, p.198). SST provides the key for unlocking the understanding of what will represent personal wins for your clients and prospects.

Chapter X

Sales Success Formula

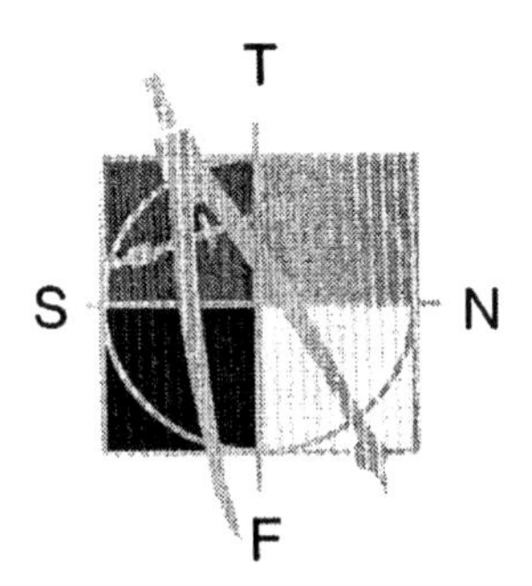

"Are you telling me that everything I was taught and have been doing for the last twenty years is wrong?"

A participant in SST raised the question when we were reciting the evidence that an emphasis on "closing" and "handling objections" actually had an adverse influence on success with major accounts. Our focus on questioning, listening and balancing value propositions didn't set well with this particular sales veteran.

While the answer to his question is a simple "yes", delivering it in a diplomatic fashion and sustaining good will with the class would be a challenge. We try to soften our reply when we field questions of that genre by indicating that, in smaller transactions, a "closing" focus might help. Further, good sales people always have a sense of next steps and "mini-sale" objectives.

Our attempts at being diplomatic while not backing away from the hard evidence that closing doesn't work in major sales, seemed to do little to mitigate the tension that was building. Then, another student rushed to our support asking people how they like being "closed" when they are buyers. Not much was the universal response.

Contrast that feeling of being manipulated into a close with a purchase you made when someone helped you solve a problem, he proposed. This prompted a dialogue about how people like to "buy solutions" and dislike being "sold". SST skills were recognized as being helpful in advancing the former while "closing" fit with the latter.

Thanks to the support of our "friend" we had an excellent experience through out the remainder of the SST program. Further, as we helped our client assess the impact of SST on performance, we were delighted to discover that sales for the team were up significantly for those using SST. In comparison, other teams in the organization who had not been taught SST showed a flat performance profile.

After examining aggregate performance for the team, the next level of inquiry was at the individual level. But for a single exception, individual performance was much higher for those using SST.

Want to guess who the exception was? If you guessed the crusty sales veteran who challenged us about the value of closing you would be wrong. It was our "friend".

Obviously, we were confused by this and curious about the explanation. What we discovered is something we have recited with every subsequent SST class we conduct.

It seems our "friend" felt so "smart" after learning SST that he stopped working hard. His level of activity in managing his pipeline dropped off precipitously the weeks following SST.

The lesson is loud and clear. Working SST smart is not enough to improve sales performance. We need to continue to work hard and perform those activities (cold calling is probably at the top of the list) that we find distasteful.

Over the years we have come-up with a formula to help us understand dynamics like those behind our "friend's" performance. It is:

Sales Performance = Skills x Motivation

The formula is multiplicative. If you remember your grade school math, you will recall that any number multiplied by zero results in zero. Basically, our "friend" made a big gain in his skill level with SST. However, his motivation to apply those skills by calling on new prospects was near zero. Consequently, he produced a near zero level performance gain.

This was a very important lesson to all involved, including our "friend". Once his manager gave him a little religion about pipeline management and daily sales disciplines, his performance skyrocketed.

The formula has been helpful diagnostically when we consult with sales leaders. Using the model of leaders as coaches, we can assess the performance issues for each person on the team. Fundamentally, the formula reinforces what coaches do. One, they help their players acquire and maintain the best <u>skills</u> possible. Two, they <u>motivate</u> their players to perform at the highest level. The principles are no different for coaching the New York Yankees than they are for coaching the sales team at I-SYS Technologies.

Skills

The skills Derek Jeter needs to excel as a shortstop are obviously different than the ones Ron McClellan's team at I-SYS requires. Since this is a book on selling and not baseball, we will focus on selling skills. Fundamentally, selling skills break down into two categories: product knowledge and selling skills.

Too many organizations make the mistake of assuming product knowledge is enough. How often have you known the smartest team member in product knowledge to also be the top performer? I have never come across a single instance, either first hand or in the literature, where this is the case.

This is not to argue that product knowledge is not important. It is. But, it is not enough.

What some refer to as the "soft" skills of selling are what can make the hard difference in competitive performance. (See "Paradox II: Soft Skills Make a Hard Difference", January 1999 newsletter, Chapter Twelve). Shamelessly, this author asserts that SST represents the best selling skill program available anywhere.

Motivation

Undergraduate psychology curricula dedicate entire courses to "Motivation". Suffice it to say that when we untangle this complicated topic, what we can do as leaders and coaches is pretty much restricted to the "rewards" we administer. Alfie Kohn (1988, p. 181) puts it as well as anyone when he writes, *"All we can do is set up certain conditions that will maximize the probability of their developing an interest in what they are doing and remove the conditions that function as constraints."*

Rewards come in two varieties: Extrinsic and Intrinsic

<u>Extrinsic Rewards</u> are the carrots at the end of the stick. They are what you "get" when you do "that". Extrinsic Rewards are always provided by someone else, tangible, and usually green. They are typically what organizations focus on when considering incentive programs

<u>Intrinsic Rewards</u>, on the other hand, come from within and are intangible. They have to do with a sense of accomplishment, pride

associated with doing a good job, learning, growing, a sense of mastery and membership.

We always encourage our clients to consider both sets of rewards, extrinsic and intrinsic. The research summarized by Rackham (1991) suggests that extrinsic rewards work only if what you want to influence has to do with people doing more of something or doing it faster. There is no evidence that extrinsic rewards have any impact on getting people to work smarter.

While it is less common for managers to consider Intrinsic Rewards, they can be more powerful than the extrinsic variety. In fact, our research on sales leaders shows that the good ones exhibit a special understanding of linking intrinsic rewards to the unique characteristics of the individuals they lead and the culture in which they function.

SST Seller Profiles. Just as there are "SST Buyer Profiles" that appear in chapters five through eight, so too are there "SST Seller Profiles". These are designed to help sales leaders understand the individual personalities comprising their team and to provide insights to unlocking peak performance. The whole question of "Sales Leadership" represents another book topic of which "Seller Profiles" will be a centerpiece. However, please feel free to give us a call (717.248.7246) or E-mail (ajtilden@tildensst.com) if you are interested in learning more about Seller Profiles in particular, or our approach to sales leadership in general.

Chapter XI

The Evolution of Selling

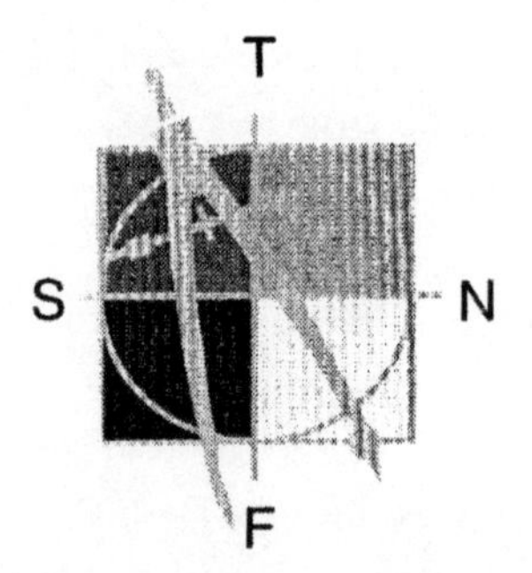

This chapter consists of SST Newsletter articles that help describe a revolution in selling. The field has moved from traditionally held and long practiced notions of manipulating "closes" with clever scripts and skills at "handling objections". Neil Rackham's monumental contribution in SPIN Selling (1988) buried those techniques under a mountain of hard scientific evidence. Still today there are many who haven't attended the manipulative selling school funeral.

The World Isn't Flat: July 1997

Quietly, there's been a revolution in selling. Like the fall of the Roman Empire, it's hard to pinpoint exactly when it started. Its origins may reach back o mid-century when counselors began to adapt the "client centered" approach ushered in by Carl Rogers. Basically, Rogers found that counselors were more effective when they focused on their clients using skills like "empathic listening". Prior to Rogers, the focus had been on the counselor and the "frame of reference" he or she had honed in graduate school.

While I can't find a precise reference, it's a safe bet that the Rogerian led revolution in counseling influenced the shift to a "consultative" approach in sales which surfaced sometime in the early 70s. Consultative practitioners began to move from a "buyer-seller" approach to building "consultant-client" relationships. Like Rogerian influenced counselors, consultative sellers focused on their clients and understanding their needs, rather than pitching features and benefits honed in product training (grad school for sales reps).

From mid-century to the turn of the century, the quiet revolution in selling has slowly, but steadily made progress. Perhaps it 's been quiet and slow because there are many in sales and sales management who haven't bought (pardon the pun) the premise that focusing on the purchaser is a superior way to approach selling. These are the sales reps in the field who can't wait to pitch their products or services and their distinctive features and benefits. Fondly, we refer to them as "show-up and throw-up" practitioners. They are the sales managers who achieved their success through working harder by pouring more prospects into the top of the funnel and memorizing thirty-two Hopkins closing scripts. Now, they write ads for sales talent with catchy headings like, "Only Closers Need Apply."

If it worked for them when they sold why shouldn't it work for those they supervise?

Neil Rackham, author of SPIN Selling, Managing Major Sales and Major Account Sales Strategy holds the answer. Through voluminous (as in studying 35,000 sales calls made by 10,000 sales reps in 27 countries) Rackham has found that there are two different universes of selling: small transactions and major sales. And, while tactics like throwing dirt on a prospect's carpet as a means of gaining "attention" (good old AIDA) may be an effective tactic if you're selling vacuum cleaners, it's hardly advisable to sabotage a hospital's air conditioning system if you represent HVAC systems for the McClure Company.

Hold onto your hats super closers, the world isn't flat. According to Rackham, "Research shows convincingly that, in larger sales at least, the use of closing techniques is negatively related to success." (Rackham, P. 122). Both SPIN and SST provide means of understanding "buyer" behaviors, which is the key to success with major account; at least among us revolutionaries.

Indeed, when the needs assessment and SST presentation stages are done well, the "close" is seamless.

Counseling & Selling: August 1997

Recently, I conducted a SST™ workshop, and as I often do, I invited the participants to offer word associations for a series of occupations: physician, accountant, engineer, CPA, lawyer, etc. I conclude the exercise by asking for associations to "counselor" and then "sales rep". Invariably, the words elicited for **counselor** are complimentary. "Listener", "helper" and "caring" are common associations. Predictably, the associations for **sales rep** are far more pejorative: "aggressive", "sleazy", and "pushy" top the list. I use this exercise to introduce an important premise upon which SST™ is based: counseling and selling require similar skills. And, when done properly, both counseling and selling follow the same three-step process.

Step One is to ask questions to help you understand the client's problem. In SST™ we teach the art of good questions, heavily influenced by the work of Neil Rackham and his SPIN model. Step Two is to listen to the responses to those questions to understand your client's problem from his or her perspective. Effective listening is essential to learning the preferred communication style of your client.

Step Three is to help the client choose a solution to solve a problem they are experiencing. The reason many in sales are held in contempt and viewed as "aggressive", "sleazy", and "pushy" is that they start at "Step Three", neglecting to ask and listen to good questions enabling them to understand their clients.

How would you feel as a client, if your counselor, fresh back from a professional conference, greeted you this way: " Boy do I have a whiz bang therapy for you. Just rolling her out and we're offering an unbelievable discount for our best customers. Would you like to schedule your sessions for Mondays or Tuesdays?"

Your clients and prospects are like you, and everyone else for that matter. They welcome understanding and genuine help for problems they are encountering. And, they resent being manipulated by a sales rep selling a solution to someone else's problem.

Listening: October 1999

Those of you have participated in SST know that we emphasize three essential skills:

1. Asking good questions
2. Listening from the perspective of the client
3. Helping the client choose a solution

Neil Rackham and his SPIN Selling (1988) has influenced us in helping our students develop good questioning skills. For skill #3, SST provides specific steps and tools to customize communication to the preferences of clients. None of this can work without the essential middle step of listening.

Planning and executing the best questions are wasted efforts if we don't listen carefully to our clients. And, customizing communication to the preferences of clients is impossible if we haven't listened to learn them. In short, without listening effectively we cannot communicate, or sell, effectively.

Although universally recognized as a crucial skill, most would agree that effective listening is too frequently absent in modern business. Our tendency is to "tell" our prospects and clients about our wonderful features, advantages and benefits before we understand them and their situation. Too often, we fail to ""*Hear the other side"* (St. Augustine*)* before we start pitching. Yet, as Chief Justice John Marshall observed:

> "To listen well is as powerful a means of communication and influence as to talk well."

Nearly two centuries later, new age guru Steven Covey popularized Marshall's wisdom with his Seven Habits of Highly Successful People. The habit pertaining most directly to selling is "Seek first to understand." To understand our prospects and clients we need to be active listeners. Once we "understand" we seek to be "understood."

Mark McCormack, author of the best selling What They Don't Teach You at Harvard Business School, understands the importance of listening. *"Business situations always come down to people situations."* The better you understand the person(s) you are dealing with the more effective you will be in selling and in business in general.

Miller and Heiman make a similar point in their New Strategic Selling. What makes this version of Strategic Selling "new" is their emphasis on "win-results". The latter relate to business gains like improved quality, efficiency, productivity and profit. "Wins" refer to "personal" gains or benefits for your prospects. Success in modern selling, they assert, can no longer rely on just business "results". We must also understand the "wins" for the people involved and harness that knowledge for our own success.

In Neil Rackham's breakthrough work on what works in modern selling, SPIN Selling, he identified the art of asking good questions as the distinguishing practice between those who succeed in consultative selling and those who fail. What we have learned from our own extensive experience in teaching consultative selling skills, is that planning and asking good questions is not enough. You must listen for both business problems as well as communication preferences.

If philosophers, statesmen, psychologists and management gurus have understood and advocated the importance of "listening" for centuries, why don't we?

What's wrong with one guy's opinion?: March 1999

Selling has been in the news. The Sunday New York Times (February 7, 1999) feature article in "Money & Business" addressed the issue of how the field has changed. The article "Salesmanship Without the Punch" features the work of James Werth and what he calls "High Probability Selling"; which by no great coincidence is the title of his book. As best I can tell, "High Probability Selling" advocates focusing your attention on probable buyers and kicking the others out of your funnel quickly.

My issue with Werth and the Times is not over the utter common sense of his approach. What prompted my letter, which they elected to publish (NYT, Money & Business, 2/28/99), is that they chose a guy like Werth for the centerpiece of the article and not Neil Rackham. What sets Rackham apart is the scientific nature of his model supported by mountains of research. SST is heavily influenced by Rackham's work with our emphasis on questioning and listening skills.

As my undergraduate adviser (Dr. John Ross) at St. Lawrence used to exhort: "If you want social opinion go down to the Tick Tock (a popular watering hole). There will be plenty of it. The later the hour the more of it. But this is about social science."

I never recall Professor Ross raising his voice, but clearly, his emphasis was on "science" and what sets it apart from one guy's opinion. And, that is what the likes of Werth and Hopkins give us: one guy's opinion.

What is wrong with one guy's opinion? Nothing when the topic is something harmless like sports. But when the business is as important as selling, relying one guy's opinion can be dangerous. After all, the guy could be wrong.

The field of selling has been rife with wrong opinions: Here's a short list:

- Close early and close often.
- The sale doesn't start until the buyer says 'no'
- Clever trial closes make a difference
- People who talk a lot excel in selling
- Handling objections makes a difference
- Any approach that treats buyers as adversaries to be manipulated into something they don't want or need

Old friend Tom Hopkins is also cited in the article which adds insult to the injury of missing Rackham. Here's what Mr. Hopkins (The Times would never use a first name) has to say: *"I couldn't wait on my butt until people came to me; I had to knock on doors."*

Pardon me Mr. Hopkins, but this isn't about working hard. The issue at hand has to do with what you do when someone answers the door. Rackham's research shows that the more sales people do what you advocate (clever closing scripts and manipulating affirmative responses to questions) the less likely they will succeed.

Relying on one guy's opinion has led to a generation of sales people doing the wrong things. From the New York Times we come to expect the very best in journalism. Who else would use a word like "verisimilitude" in a business article?

We should get more than one guy's opinion from the New York Times. There are plenty of those at the local pub. However, quality research on selling is as rare as bad syntax in a William Safire column.

Duh: November 1998

Robert Eaton, CEO of Chrysler is quoted in a "rare" September 28 interview with USA TODAY, *"Something on the order of 65% of customers don't like the car buying process . . . If they don't like it we better change."*

His interpretation is that today's car shoppers are smarter technically because they search the internet prior to visiting a car lot.

The solution says Jack Smith, CEO of GM, is to bring the sales organization *"to a higher level of technical expertise."*

If I were still teaching research methods, I would use this as a classic example of misinterpreting data. The reason customers don't like the car buying process is not because the sales force lacks product knowledge. **It is because of how they are treated when they shop for cars.**

Duh.

Pardon me, Robert and Jack, but you are barking up the wrong tree. Have your sales force ask good questions. Emphasize listening instead of pitching features like rack and pinion steering (anybody know what it is?) Then teach them to communicate in the preferred style of the client.

Finally, terminate the first sales person who refers to a client as "Pal", "Buddy" or "Hon".

Chapter XII

SST in Practice

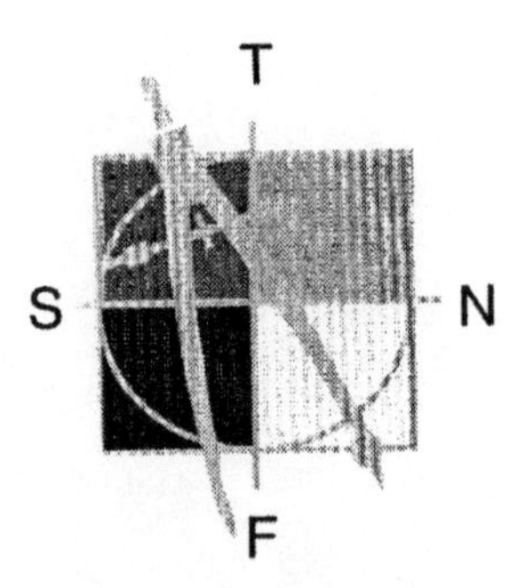

The collection of articles in this chapter is principally targeted for those already practicing the program and seeking to reinforce and improve their skills. They also somewhat shamelessly extol the virtues of SST for those considering various sales education options.

What Distinguishes SST: October 1997

I'm probably not telling you something you don't already know when I refer to *other* selling models which are designed to help the seller recognize different personalities or styles with their clients. After all, the premise that we are not all alike makes such common sense, someone had to try to develop a system for recognizing those differences to improve sales performance. They have.

They are out there. Perhaps you have heard of DISC, or Drivers, Amiables, Assertives or Actors, Friends, Doers and Thinkers, or VITOS and Seymours. I suspect there are others.

What sets SST apart? you may ask. **Difference number one** is that SST is anchored in Carl Jung's theory of personality types. Jung, as you likely know, first wrote on personality in the late 1920s and since then his theory has been thoroughly researched and carefully validated. SST goes beyond opinion and the experiences of one person in sales turned trainer and then author. That's what's wrong with *Selling to VITO.* It's based on the author's experiences and his alone. It falls into the Tom Hopkins, "This worked for me. Therefore, it will work for you." approach. The key question for them is "Where are your data when you claim that I will find a VITO here or a Seymour there?"

Which leads us to **difference number two**: we can give you those data. The SST model is supported by five decades of research, much of it done with the Myers Briggs Type Indicator, on practical applications of Jung's theory. What this means is that when we assert that 9 of 10 lawyers are **NT** types, or that 9 of 10 bankers are **ST**'s, we can give you the citations for those studies.

Difference number three is that SST is both supported by voluminous academic research *and* it is practically proven. While it's founder, yours truly, holds an academic doctorate, I also have walked in your moccasins for more than a decade. Russ Brooks, who often co-facilitates SST workshops, has been in sales for thirty years.

And, finally, **difference number four** is that SST works. We can prove it.

SST & SPIN: A Paradox: October 1997

Practitioners of SST™ know that one of the essential tools for understanding the client's business and personality is asking good questions. We have been heavily influenced by the work of Neil Rackham and the SPIN model he has advanced. Fundamentally, he found that the questioning process is an extremely powerful selling behavior. **S** stands for **Situation** questions, which gather basic information about the client and his or her business. They ask, "What have you got?" **P** or **Problem** questions probe for dissatisfaction, difficulties and disappointments. "If you could improve three things about your current service, what would they be?"

I or **Implications** questions separate the adults from the children in successful selling by asking about the consequences or implications of a problem. "The last time your network went down, could you tell me the effect it had on productivity? Morale? Overtime? Lost opportunities?" Finally, **N** or **Needs Payoff** Questions ask about the positive value of solving a problem. "What would it mean to your business if your network went down less frequently?"

Fundamentally, that's SPIN. Conceptually it is simple. Ask these questions. You can even write them down before your interview. Indeed, you should write them down. In most interviews it is even O.K. to refer to the questions and to take notes. It's empirically proven that if you ask these questions, especially with major accounts, you will have a greater probability of succeeding.

Yet, we consistently find that asking SPIN questions is difficult. Jeff Frank of Dun & Bradstreet put it this way, "SPIN is easy to say. But, it's hard to do."

Conceptually, the Successful Selling to Type SST model is far more challenging. It's anchored in Carl Jung's theory of personality types. And, while we emphasize the four communication styles of ST (Stabilizers), SF (Communicators), NF (Catalysts) & NT (Visionaries) there are as many as sixteen personality types.

While Rackham and his colleagues have followed *SPIN Selling* with *Major Account Sales Strategy, Managing Major Sales* and *Getting Partnering Right* (all published by McGraw Hill) there are hundreds of publications on Jung's work and its applications to counseling, team building and education. Successful Selling to Type: SST is unique in applying Jung's model to selling.

And herein lies an interesting paradox. SST, although more difficult intellectually, is easier to learn and to implement. In a recent follow-up assessment with a client we asked, along with nine other questions, "Have you found any parts of SST difficult to apply? Which ones?" Head-and-shoulders, the SPIN component of SST stood out as the most difficult one to use in the field. Here are some representative comments:

"Sometimes the interview just takes off and I don't get to ask the questions I planned."
"The SPIN process doesn't always flow the way you want it to."
"SPIN doesn't always apply."

Okay, you ask," So what does it mean?" It could simply be that asking questions, of any nature, is more difficult than offering our views. In school, and probably most homes, we are rewarded for the answers we give rather than the questions we ask or the understanding we achieve. Thus, when we get into sales where, instead of letter grades and gold stars, we are seeking commissions and compensation, we tend to give answers. After all, that's what we have been taught.

New age Guru Steven Covey addresses this issue in his *Seven Habits of Highly Successful People.* Seek first to understand, he asserts. Then, seek to be understood. In the SST model, Rackham's SPIN is essential to thorough understanding of the client's business problems and his or her preferred communications style. In SST, we employ SPIN when we are seeking to understand.

Then, when we are seeking to be understood, we communicate in the preferred language of our client. SPIN may be easy to say but hard to do. But, it's clearly worth learning.

LD

SST & Four Buyer Influences: December 1997

In what feels like a lifetime ago, I was team teaching a college course on Counseling Theories. After studying the likes of Ellis, Freud, Jung, Perls and Rogers we observed that, in practice, many counselors drew from the different models. They might shift from being very Rogerian and long term with one client while being quite directive and Ellis like with another. We referred to this practice as being "eclectic".

The final evaluation had both a written component and an interview with a member of the teaching team. Just by the luck of the draw, I got to do the oral exam with one of our "favorite" students. I asked him, if he were to enter the counseling field that very day, what would his approach be? He responded, "Well, Dr. Tilden, I guess you could call my counseling style epileptic."

As I choked back the coffee I made the mistake of sipping, I thought to myself, "He's probably right".

This anecdote about counseling theories is apropos because the central premise of SST is that the processes of counseling and selling are fundamentally alike. Moreover, SST is "eclectic" in scope. We build on Neil Rackham's SPIN to assess, not only business problems and their implications, but to learn the personality types of our clients and prospects in the context of Carl Jung's theory. Once we have "sought to understand", ala Stephen Covey, we "seek to be understood" by communicating in the preferred Jungian language of the buyer.

In each of the previous three SST Newsletters we have referenced Rackham's SPIN. There is yet another important work that SST draws upon which, heretofore, has gone unmentioned: Strategic Selling. First published in 1985, the 1998 version, The New Strategic Selling by Heiman et al. is just out.

Veterans of SST may not remember the citation, but will certainly recall the *Four Buyers: Economic, User, Technical & Coach.* The *Economic Buyer* controls the purse strings of an organization and gives final approval. Increasingly, *Economic Buyers* are consulting with *User and Technical* Buyers before signing off. *User Buyers* are the people who will actually be using your product or service. They (and there's usually more than one) will assess its impact on how it will help them do their jobs. *Technical Buyers* cannot say, "yes" to a purchase. But, they can say "no" if it doesn't satisfy the technical specifications of which they are custodians. Finally, Heiman's model preaches the virtues of having a *"Coach"* who wants to see you succeed and often provides an insider's perspective to essential buying dynamics of the client organization.

SST steps and tools are not just applied to a single buyer. Influenced by Heiman et al. and Strategic Selling, we apply it to all four buying influences. The Four-Buyer model is consistent with SST because it emphasizes planning an "account centered" strategy for every client rather than using the same "seller centered" tactics on every call. We have fondly referred to the latter as the "show-up and throw-up" school of selling.

If you pick up The New Strategic Selling ($15 from Warner Books), I suggest that you go directly to chapter ten where the major revision appears: "Win-Results". This concept is also complementary to SST. In fact, we have incorporated similar principles into SST for some time.

Fundamentally, "Win-Results" differentiates between a business R*esult* (greater productivity, improved efficiencies more profit, etc.) and a W*in* that is personal (positive recognition from superiors, more leisure, less stress, improved status with staff etc.). Heiman et al. (p.198) now assert that, "It's never enough to sell Results alone."

SST provides the key to unlocking the understanding of what will be a "Win" for different buyers. They are as varied as the different personality type comprising the SST model.

Preparing Holiday Turkeys: November 1998

Sensing Instructions (Influenced by Bonnie Marsh's "Pumpkin Soup")

Ingredients:
One 16 lb. turkey
¼ cup of celery
¼ cup of butter
1 teaspoon of basil
2 tablespoons chopped onions
¾ cup of salt
4 cups of crustless day-old bread
½ teaspoon of paprika
¼ cup of parsley 2 eggs

Set out all the necessary equipment: measuring cups, sharpened knives, calipers, thermometer, oven rack, and assorted pots and pans.

Go down the list of ingredients placing a check mark (✓) next to each item.

Preheat oven to precisely 450° Fahrenheit.

While preheating oven, use a carpenters level to double check your measuring surface. Shim leveling surfaces as required.

Follow step-by-step instructions in Joy of Cooking (1984, p. 352) to prepare dressing.

Place the stuffing into the turkey's cavity.

Place the turkey on a rack, uncovered.

Put bird in oven and immediately reduce heat to 350° Fahrenheit.

Baste every fifteen minutes.

Cover turkey after 30 minutes.

Cook for 6 hours and 36 minutes.

Serve

Intuitive Instructions

Although obviously North American in its origins, the turkey has become a global bird with many rich traditions for preparation. Possibilities for how you prepare this year's turkey are endless. Let your imagination guide you to an exciting new holiday tradition that will be the envy of family and neighbors.

When you begin to shop for your turkey, allow yourself to contemplate the implications of electronic commerce on this holiday tradition. Don't miss the entrepreneurial opportunity you have been seeking. Why not become www.turkey.com providing this healthy white meat year round to cost conscious consumers? Allow time now to do an internet search because this is a far more exciting idea than preparing one measly bird.

Now that you are back from your search and resigned to the kitchen, we need to prepare the turkey. Stuffing is an excellent time to empty the refrigerator and cabinets. While preheating the oven (or starting the barbecue fire) hunt for onions, sausage, celery, stale bread, rice, ham, nuts, potatoes, apples, oranges etc.

Substitutions for this list are encouraged. Your creativity may be enhanced by a glass of white wine (or a nice Merlot for that matter). Now go to your spice rack, pick out your favorites and sprinkle liberally over the stuffing.

Cook until golden brown and serve. NB. Whenever your guests ask if they can "bring something", answer "yes". Have them serve the other courses. Enjoy.

Thinking Instructions

An organized approach to the preparation of the turkey always pays dividends. Prepare a list of the desired outcomes in advance of the celebration and then plan the best way to accomplish them. Be analytical in your approach. For example, if one of the desired outcomes is seeing family and another is not making a mess of the house, consider going out to dinner. If you are going to celebrate at home, can you leave relatives with kids off the guest list? If you have to invite kids, can you serve them in the garage? Consider costs and benefits of all of the angles.

Let's face it. Lions, Cowboys, Packers and Vikings have become as much a part of holidays as, say, the Pilgrims. Plan the meal accordingly. Pick the games that are "must see" and be certain to have the meal completed in advance.

Look for efficiencies both in purchasing and preparing the bird. Turkey is hard to beat on price so resist suggestions about expensive seafood as an alternative. Store brand products work as well as expensive name brands in the stuffing. Leftovers are great, but even turkey gets old after a week. Know how many people you will be serving before you make purchases. Why not get a caterer to bid the job and then prorate the fee over all the guests? This could be the way to go, even if you may have to make allowances for kids who don't eat much.

Feeling Instructions

The principal focus in preparing a holiday turkey is, of course, your guests. In addition to family, why not invite someone less fortunate to your table this year?

If you don't know any unfortunate souls first-hand, another humane way to celebrate the holiday is to volunteer the entire family to work a shift at your nearest soup kitchen. Ask Uncle Al to have his limousine service pick everyone up, wait while you work your shift, and then drive you back to your home.

Turkey, at least, is a white meat. However, many are raised and eventually slaughtered under inhumane conditions. Knowing the history of your turkey is as important today as it was to know about California grapes in the 60s.

Finally, you will need to be sensitive to both the tastes and the values of your guests. A good way to be sure you are not serving anything offensive is to circulate a "Prohibited Foods" list before the holiday. Consider a vegetarian celebration this year. Whatever you serve, make sure everyone feels welcome and warm. That, after all, is what holidays are about.

Selling Malpractice: March 1999

Late last summer we began incorporating an exercise into SST called, "You are the counselor". Simply, we pair people up to respond to this circumstance: "*You are a counselor on a college campus. A faculty acquaintance calls to inform you that she has asked a student to make an appointment with you. It has been arranged for tomorrow at 2. The background is that the new semester has brought with it a sharp change in behavior with the student you will be seeing. Last semester, he made every class, contributed actively and earned a respectable grade. This semester his attendance is spotty, his appearance disheveled and he failed the first hourly exam. How you would prepare for tomorrow's appointment?"*

Uniformly, the groups report planning questions to try to pinpoint the problem. Playing the role of counselor, they recognize that problems could reside in one or more arenas. There could be health problems. Or, the student may be having problems at home. Could it be a broken romance or a roommate rift? Another common suggestion is to talk with other professors to see if this represents a pattern or an isolated circumstance.

Notably, no one suggests proposing a solution, or planning a pitch, until the problem has been thoroughly investigated and understood. It would be unthinkable to meet the client and begin by outlining the features, advantages and benefits of a new girlfriend. How would a counselor be received who met this hypothetical appointment by proposing a little Ritalin from the friendly campus health center? Or, how about a good old "shape up kid or you'll flunk out" lecture. These practices would clearly be grounds for counseling malpractice.

Yet, most students will acknowledge that they have conducted their pre-SST selling in an analogous way. Planning for a call has meant polishing a presentation. Investigations are often truncated and predetermined to uncover a problem your product or service could solve.

The moral is to plan your sales calls just the way you would plan to meet a counseling client. Learn as much as you possibly can before the call. Plan questions to help you and your client pinpoint problem areas. Listen carefully. Then help the client choose a solution communicated in his or her preferred style. Anything else is grounds for malpractice.

Avoiding the FAB Trap: July 1998

Practitioners of SST know the steps well. The acronym is PIDO, which stands for Preliminaries, Investigating, Demonstrating Capability and Obtaining Commitment. While PIDO corresponds to Rackham's SPIN selling, it is completely compatible with other models emphasizing a needs assessment, seeking first to understand (Covey) or "opening" the sale (Gerber).

At the core are the middle two steps of Investigating and Demonstrating Capability. Step One, Preliminaries should be kept brief. Step Four, Obtaining Commitment is the ultimate reason for the call and where the financial incentives lie. When Steps Two and Three are done well, Obtaining Commitment is seamless and natural.

Steps Two and Three are the skill steps. It is where we focus when we teach SST. The Investigation is modeled after Rackham's SPIN. SST, however, not only uncovers business problems and their implications, but also identifies communication preferences of prospects. When we Demonstrate Capability, Step Three, we propose solutions in the preferred language of the prospect or client.

Whenever I describe SST, I feel that Step Three sounds more difficult than Step Two. Repeatedly, however, our evaluations show that people have more difficulty with Step Two, the SPIN Investigation.

As someone who not only teaches SST, but who uses it, I think I have an insight to offer. Perhaps you are falling prey to the FAB Trap. If you have had an experience like the one I am about to describe, you have.

Preparing for an important call, you dutifully prepare your SPIN questions on your SST Account Worksheet. Preliminaries are completed and you begin with your Situation questions. Your prospects look uncomfortable. When you move to Problem questions they start fidgeting.

Finally, one of your prospects interrupts the SPIN by saying something like, "We know our problems. That is why we are here. We would like to hear what you and XYZ, Inc. could do to help us solve them."

Boom. SPIN is over. You move into pitching FABs (Features, Advantages and Benefits) which is probably a more comfortable zone for both you and your client.

Sound familiar? It sometimes happens to me. It is the FAB Trap. If you fall for it, you can look worse than the guys who have Bitter Beer Face.

Here is a solution I propose. Sometimes it is necessary to do a "Mini Demonstration of Competency". The purpose is to gain permission to conduct the full SPIN. Give them some FAB and make the transition back to SPIN by saying something like, "XYZ has been able to help many firms like yours. Our solutions, however, look different because while similar, no two firms are exactly alike. It would help me if I could understand your firm more fully. Then, we can help you customize a solution." If you can, restart your SPIN with an issue or problem they volunteered. "Can you walk me through what happened the last time you had that problem?"

The FAB Trap is quite enticing. It feels comfortable. Most of us would rather talk than listen. However, listening is essential to understanding your prospect. The better you understand your prospects, the more sales successes you will enjoy.

Sighted Squirrels Find More Nuts: March 1998

"Are you telling us everything we have been taught is wrong?" This is

not an unfamiliar refrain when doing an SST workshop. Sometimes we're tempted to respond, "Well, yes." However, that wouldn't be perfectly accurate. While there are some necessary and important traditional selling techniques, there are others that should be discarded from modern major account selling.

Old school selling went something like this: *Prospect, Qualify, Demonstrate, Trial Close, Handle Objections, Close.* The process starts with the essential sales behaviors known as "Prospecting" and "Qualifying". They are 95% will and 5% skill. Both are absolutely essential selling behaviors. After all, if you don't have a qualified prospect, you can't make a sale.

It is once we get in front of a prospect, however, that differences between "Old School" and "SST" selling surface. The old school emphasizes a demonstration that wows the prospect with the latest and greatest FAB (Features, Advantages and Benefits). It is followed by the infamous *trial close.* "Would you like your first order, Monday or Friday?"

If they say neither, the old school seller is driven by the single phrase that has done more to produce obnoxious sales behavior than any other, "The sale doesn't begin until your prospect says 'no'". Undaunted by the first "no", the old school seller *handles the objection* with something like, "I can appreciate that sentiment, however if you will sign today, we can save you considerable money on the cost of shipping."

If a skillful *handling of objections* doesn't work, the poor prospect is in for an endless series of *closes.* Students of Tom Hopkins memorize thirty plus closing scripts. If the Ben Franklin doesn't work, hit them with the Puppy Dog. Ad nauseam.

SST is based on the premise that effective sales people have much in common with good counselors. Both ask good questions. Then, they listen attentively to responses. Once they understand the problem from the perspective of the client, they help him or her choose a solution. They take care to communicate in the preferred style of the client. In other words, they don't walk in pitching what they happen to have in the trunk of the car.

Step one *Preliminaries* should be brief. It's important to warm the call up. But be ready to get down to business, early. Step two, the *Investigation,* is crucial and modeled after Neil Rackham's SPIN system. With SST, we not only uncover business problems and their implications, we also learn the preferred way the client would like to see *Capability* demonstrated, which is step three.

When the *Investigation* and *Demonstration of Capability* are done well, the "close" is seamless. It doesn't require tricks and manipulation. *Obtaining Commitment* flows naturally when the client is understood and communication is in his or her preferred style.

But, in order for SST to payoff you still need qualified prospects to interview. And, this is what Old School" selling and SST have in common. The world's greatest SST practitioner will not make sales without prospects to interview. Conversely, an annoying schlepper using manipulative techniques will still make sales if he or she has lots of prospects to interview. Blind squirrels find nuts.

Prospecting and qualifying are matters of "will". If your sales team has the "will" to prospect and you give them the "skill" of SST your sales will increase; perhaps as dramatically as Penn State Geisinger Health Plan's. After all, sighted squirrels find more nuts.

What if Willie Loman, Blake & Lou Gehrig Had Power Point?: May 1999

"Death of a Salesman" is back on Broadway starring Brian Dennehey as Willie Loman. Ever wonder what poor Willie's selling techniques would be like today, roughly a half-century after Arthur Miller wrote the famous play? He'd certainly be armed with more than the product samples he lugged around in his tired old brief case. Today's Willie would carry a lap top computer. And, you guessed it, that lap top would be programmed with a Microsoft Power Point presentation promoting his product line.

Indeed, all an Information Age Willie would need to do is click on the "Wizard" in Power Point and choose "Presenting a Product or Service". Then, step-by-step, Microsoft partner Dale Carnegie will lead him through one of their "High Impact" presentations.

In order, Willie's slides would be titled: Product Name, Overview, Features & Benefits, Applications, Specifications, Pricing & Availability. Each slide appears on Willie's choice of a richly hued background with the main point supported by just the right number of bullets appearing in the recommended font and style. Willie can switch his brain off and let Microsoft and Dale Carnegie do his thinking for him.

The less famous, but to me even more compelling theatrical figure of sales, is Blake of David Mamet's Glengarry Glen Ross. Immortalized by Alec Baldwin on screen, I wonder how Blake would incorporate technology into his motivational talks?

"Put that coffee down! Coffee is for closers.

Mitch & Murray sent me here because you guys aren't using your Power Points.

(Answering Ed Harris) Why me? Because my Power Point presentations helped me make $950,000 last year. How much did you make?

I could go out tonight with the Power Point presentation you got and make $15,000! (To Alan Arkin) Could you?

A guy don't let you open your lap top lest he wants to buy. (To Lemmon) Are you man enough to make him sit through the slides?

Now, let me show you tonight's Power Point on:

Slide One: "This Month's Sales Contest"

Slide Two: "First place is a Cadillac"

Slide Three: "Second prize . . . a set of steak knives"

Slide Four: "Third prize. . . . You're fired"

Oh, did my Power Point get your attention . . .

Oh yes, the ubiquitous Power Point. Hasn't it done for presentations what word processing did for written communication? That is, make them easy to prepare in a professional looking fashion.

Applying a SST lens helps us see the limitations of Power Point presentations. While they appeal to Sensors of the population they can be a bad fit for those of who prefer Intuition for taking in information. Sensors like information that is presented in a step-by-step fashion loaded with specific facts and figures. Knowing that they will get to pricing in slide six, will put them at ease.

On the other hand, Intuitive types like to be free to make associations, or Intuitive leaps. During slide four's "Applications", they may want to explore novel ways of using your product and not want to go immediately to "Specifications" in slide five.

Power Point presentations not only numb the creativity characteristic of Intuitives, but they are also devoid of the emotional connection important to Feeling preferred decision makers. Can you imagine if New York Yankee immortal Lou Gehrig had used Power Point for his famous farewell?

For those of you who aren't baseball fans, Gehrig batted clean up behind Babe Ruth on what most consider the greatest team of all time. Nicknamed the "Iron Horse", Gehrig contracted what is now commonly known as Lou Gehrig's disease. With Yankee Stadium awash in tears the stricken Gehrig told his adoring fans, *"Today, I am the luckiest man on the face of the earth. I may have been given a bad break. But, I have an awful lot to live for. Thank you"*

A 90's Gehrig, assisted by Power Point, would use the electronic scoreboard to flash a series of slides listing his career .340 batting average, his fielding statistics, and his record for 2130 consecutive games played. The "Pride of the Yankees" would never be a movie and Gary Cooper would be denied his greatest part.

While Thinking preferred decision makers will zero in on itemized "Benefits", dimming the lights for a Power Point shuts down the opportunity to build a personal connection important to many who prefer "Feelings" for their decision making. While you may never approach the emotion of Gehrig's farewell, Power Point presentations do limit your opportunity to stir the heart.

At the risk of being misunderstood, I am not contending that Power Point should never be used. In fact, it is a good fit with the ST "Stabilizer" types who are heavily represented in traditional management positions. SST facilitator Russ Brooks has good success, for example, using Power Point with bankers. "Banking is an ST environment. Power Point works well there but I use other SST methods in other settings."

The premise of SST is that communication effectiveness is the key to selling. Power Point can be a good tool if your target consists of people preferring the ST language. Successful Selling to Type suggests more effective communication styles for the other three languages: SF, NF and NT.

Rethinking the Sales Force: May 1999 by Neil Rackham & John DeVincentis

Neil Rackham brings to selling what Galileo brought to exploration: a little science. More than a decade ago, Rackham and his research team conducted a monumental study by investigating 35,000 sales calls to identify successful selling behaviors. The findings he reported in SPIN Selling (McGraw Hill, 1988). were considered as heretical as early assertions that the world is not flat.

Hold on to your hats if you still believe that slick closing techniques and handling objections make the difference in major account selling. Not only is the world round, but thanks to Rackham's research we have learned that the more closing tactics you exhibit the less likely it is that you will succeed. Instead, he discovered that the most compelling selling behavior is the question.

The formulation of a method for investigating client needs is the central contribution of Rackham's landmark SPIN Selling. Since then, Rackham has been the principal author for these other helpful contributions to the field of sales: Major Account Sales Strategy (McGraw Hill, 1989), Managing Major Sales (Harper, 1991) and Getting Partnering Right (McGraw Hill, 1996).

In a Sunday edition of "Money & Business" The New York Times featured an article called, "Breaking the Mold: Salesmanship Without the Sucker Punch" (2/7/99). Disappointed that they did not give Rackham credit for his pioneering work, I sent a letter off to their editor which they chopped in half and then published (2/28/99). In appreciation, Rackham sent me a gracious reply and a complimentary copy of his just published, Rethinking the Sales Force (McGraw-Hill, 1999).

If, like many of our clients, you are trying to figure out how to sell value when your buyers are shopping for commodity like prices, Rethinking the Sales Force is a must read. Helpfully, Rackham provides insights from the buyer's perspective which, after all, is the only way we can learn how to *add* value. Simply *communicating* value, he correctly asserts, is no longer enough.

From Rethinking the Sales Force we learn that buyers are embracing a model called "strategic buying programs". Herein they weigh two variables: strategic importance and difficulty of substitution for the supplier's product or service. If your product or service is perceived as offering low strategic importance and competes against easy to find alternatives, be prepared for a commodity mentality.

Thankfully, Rackham does more than explain how we can fall in to a commodity trap. He also helps us sellers plan our most effective strategy to get out. The one-size fits all approach won't cut it in today's market place. Multiple selling strategies offer the key to success.

Balance & Shade: April 2000

Each time we teach SST, an astute observer will raise the question of the difficulty of "typing" a prospect accurately. They say something like:

"My God, I wasn't even sure of my own type after going through SST and having taken the MBTI. How in the world can I type someone else accurately? Especially in the context of a sales call, when I'm trying to remember to ask good questions and listen. Let alone all of the technical expertise I need to bring to the table."

SST is one of those programs where the process is as important as the outcome. That is to say, the mere process of using the SST tools to identify preferences of a client is valuable all by itself. They discipline us to put the focus of the process where it should be: on the buyer. And, if you can't type someone, it doesn't matter.

Doesn't matter? Yes, it doesn't matter because ensuring that your messages, stories and value propositions are balanced will enhance your communication effectiveness. When you are unsure of a client's preferences, your communication effectiveness can still be significantly increased by "balancing" your communication.

Balance

Balance simply requires understanding your own preferences and natural tendency to emphasize them in communication. To be balanced means making certain that you are sending Intuitive as well as Sensing messages and Feeling as well as Thinking messages.

Having provided the assurance that SST is really goof-proof, we would like to add that our experience shows that most times prospects and clients will "scream" their preferences. Roughly, this is what we find 8 times out of 10.

Even when someone shouts, "I am a Sensing Thinker", we don't advise sending exclusive "Sensing-Thinking" kinds of messages. One reason is that intellectually capable people like the buyers and buyer influences you encounter require information that appeals to all four of the mental functions. Therefore, even when someone's preferences are crystal clear, we advise that you "shade" your communication.

Shade

Shade means giving information that appeals to the client's preferences first, and following with the other function. In other words, if you are certain you have a Sensor, start with the facts and details before describing the big picture and future benefits. If you are with a "Thinker", give her the "logic to buy" first. Then, make your "Feeling" oriented points about the positive impact on people.

Don't Type During the Call

Finally, to those of you alarmed about having too much to do during a sales call, we hope to comfort you with the observation that we don't recommend that you "type" during the call. Recall that our objective is to conduct a dialogue with the client and not appear like we are doing a psychological profile.

What we do advice, is that as soon after the call as possible, run through the Behavioral Cues Worksheets found in the SST Binder. Or, you can use a SST Planning Folder to record your impressions. Ask yourself, "What did I see?" Place a check mark next to each phrase that fits. This discipline will be rewarded many times over.

My Mentor & Friend, Ron Cherry: April 2000

My mentor and friend Ron Cherry died this week. Over the years, most of you have heard me refer to "My Mentor', although rarely by name. In the introduction to SST, I tell the story about how I was introduced to consulting by a faculty colleague who invited me to apply the Myers Briggs Type Indicator to help his client improve teamwork. That introduction was the impetus to my consulting career and eventually the development of SST, a selling relative to the MBTI.

Others have heard me reference Ron when a tough organizational question came my way. I'd say something like, "Let me check with Ron Cherry who has been my mentor over the years. He is just the brightest guy I know on matters like this."

With an exchange of E-mails followed by an early lunch at Tops Diner, (*"Brand loyalty, you know"*) Ron would offer insights that were just brilliant. Before "thinking outside the box" became a buzzword, Ron had it down to an art form. Before "client centered" thinking or "Customer Relationship Management' became trends, Ron was demonstrating those principles. He was consistently years ahead of the management curve.

Perhaps you recall my reference to Ron when I have encouraged your team to challenge creeping "group think". *"Being a team does not mean agreeing all the time."*

Once, I backed down from a position because Ron made a more compelling case. To which he responded, *"If we agree, one of us is redundant."*

Another time, I recited the famous Thorndike quote to Ron. "If it exists", I said, "it can be measured." Ron replied, *"If you can measure it, it probably doesn't matter."*

Simply, Ron was the best teacher I ever saw and the brightest guy I ever met. He saw things no one else could. I will always be indebted to him and aspire to the standards he set.

SST for Scandinavia June-July 2000

It started in April of 1999 with an E-mail with the intriguing title, "SST for Scandinavia". With great curiosity I opened it and read an introduction from Rolf Dackheden of the Human Management Foundation indicating an interest in learning more about SST. He described Human Management as a foundation of fifteen consultants who specialize in sales education, marketing, team building and leadership training. Three of the consultants, he noted, were certified in the MBTI (a paper-and-pencil instrument based on the same personality theory as SST). Their clients include marquee names like: Volvo, Saab, Ericsson, Ikea and Swedish Telecom.

Rolf framed our internet dialogue with questions like:

- What have you accomplished with the concept?
- What kinds of clients have had the most success?
- What kinds of instruments do you use?
- Have you done assessments to track results?
- Do you use the MBTI?

As I responded with various reports, studies and newsletter articles to explain SST and the terrific results it delivers, Rolf's questions became more focused:

- Having already used and taught NLP and SPIN, what makes SST different?
- How is it better?

I responded by describing the success we have enjoyed by building on SPIN to, not only to identify business problems and their implications, but the style preferences of the "people" involved in the business.

Concerning NLP, SST is simply based on a richer more respected theory and supported by empirical evidence NLP lacks. This led to the pivotal question, "What would be necessary to train us to use SST in Scandinavia?"

The next step was for Rolf and one of his partners, Peter Larsson, to visit with us in October when the colors in the beautiful mountains of central Pennsylvania are at their peak. We spent three exciting days together reviewing SST training films and learning from one another in the context of the fascinating work we do. Russ Brooks and Inge Olson added to our lively exchanges. Socially, we feasted on great food, single malt scotch provided by our guests, and took an afternoon to visit the Amish Farmers market held in nearby Big Valley.

At the conclusion of Rolf and Peter's autumn visit we agreed to proceed with what they term a "Business Cooperation", a phrase that sounds far more synergistic than "license" or "contract". Specifically, we agreed that Rolf and Peter would do their "homework" on the growth points we identified and then demonstrate their SST competencies for me. This would lead to their formal certification in the program.

Roughly one year from the start of our internet dialogue, we visited with Rolf and Peter, staying with Rolf and his family on the beautiful peninsula where they live. We spent a memorable weekend preparing for Monday and Tuesday's SST delivery to an engineering firm. Our work time was nicely broken up with delicious fresh seafood, castle tours and wonderful hospitality.

Although everyone is fluent in English, our joint assessment was that the best understanding of SST would be achieved if it were to be delivered in the client's native tongue. Some idioms just don't travel well. A "seasoned sales person" would be one that might taste good to a cannibal. The "Show–up and Throw-up" sales call, against which we contrast a thorough SST investigation, translates to, "Be there and vomit". Swedish was the way to go.

Peter had translated the SST materials and he and Rolf provided periodic translations for me as the sessions progressed. This enhanced my general recognition of how the program was unfolding from following our slides that support the SST teaching and learning process.

Peter and Rolf did great and the client proved to be thirsty to learn. There were no distractions from cell phones or pagers. Time boundaries on breaks were strictly honored. I could tell that there was excellent give and take among teachers and students.

I don't know how the "proof is in the pudding" might translate, but there was plenty of it (proof that is) that SST was a huge hit with the client. By the time I got back to the states I had this E-mail awaiting me from Rolf:

"*We have received spontaneous telephone calls from our participants who all are very positive. The group leader (sic) told me that the normally most critical person had said that it was the* best *education he had ever taken part in!! He told me that he used the SST in his discussion with his area manager the day after the seminar. The discussion ended with his area manager suggesting that he go ahead with the group. He got carte blanche from his manager on his own initiative! It works really!*

Another participant (sic) used his new knowledge in his education the day after with very good results. Yet another (sic) is even sending the word around. When he is on sales calls he markets SST. He has already given me names to contact for the SST program. Great isn't it?"

In a word, it is great. It is great to harness the genius of Carl Jung and to find such wonderful business partners and international friends. Rolf and Peter, well done! Skoal!

Chapter XIII

Sales Leadership

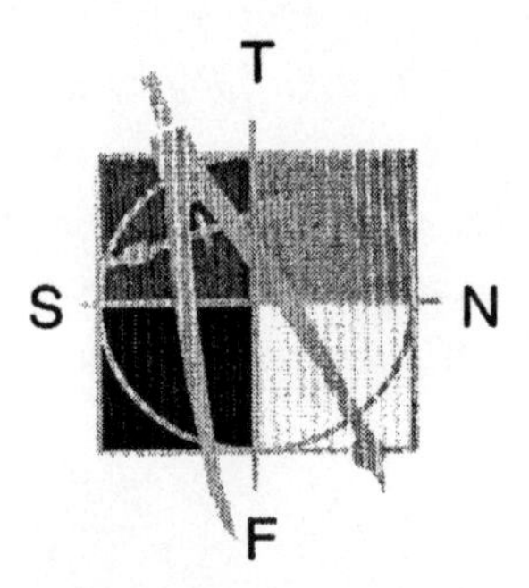

There can be no sustained improvement in sales performance without effective sales leadership. As SST evolved, it was quite natural to extend the notions of self-understanding and communication effectiveness to the relationships a sales leader cultivates with his or her team.

Lombardi on Leadership: February 2000

Since "coaching" is a model that we use for developing sales leadership skills, we are always interested in learning more about great coaches. When David Maraniss' When Pride Still Mattered appeared on the New York Times best seller list, it immediately registered as a must read. Maraniss is a Pulitzer Prize winning writer for The Washington Post. His subject is the legendary coach of the Green Bay Packers.

What we can learn about leadership from the coach who guided his team to victory in the first Super Bowl, not only transcends sports, but is still relevant as the countdown to Super Bowl thirty-four is underway.

Know your players

"There are other coaches who know more about X's and O's," Lombardi once remarked. "But I've got an edge. I know more about football players than they do."

Use different motivational strategies for different players

Guard Jerry Kramer once joked, "*Lombardi treated us all the same, like dogs.*" It's a funny line that wasn't true. The part about being treated the same, anyway. He knew that players like Paul Hornung didn't mind being taken to task during practice. Others like Willie Davis and Fuzzy Thurston couldn't stand being singled out. Accordingly, he would blast Hornung anytime he screwed-up (usually for being late for curfews) and talk privately with Davis and Thurston.

Quarterback Bart Starr was one of those who preferred private conversations. He approached Lombardi and told him he felt his leadership effectiveness was undermined whenever he got his butt chewed at practice. From then on, Lombardi held his tongue and reserved all of his concerns for quarterback to coach talks. Starr's performance took off and the Packers started to win.

Lombardi had an uncanny knack for "reading" people. SST provides a model for all leaders to improve their understanding of their "players". There are also "tools" for customizing communication and reward strategies.

Use rewards that fit the culture

Selling and football have a lot in common. In fact, Lombardi once appeared in a film on that subject. One of the big differences, however, is that game day performance on the football field is recorded on film. Lombardi and his staff would break down the performance of every player on every play and grade it as a zero, one or two.

Lombardi then conducted an "Awards Ceremony" and called the names of the players with the highest ratings and most improvement to the front of the room. There he would pull crisp bills form his wallet and pass them out to the honorees. The amount of the bills? First five and eventually ten dollars.

What mattered was what the ceremony represented in the culture: being recognized for doing an excellent job by your boss in front of your peers. The money was secondary. Tight end Gary Knafelc said, *"It was amazing how prideful you would become. It could have been five thousand dollars it meant so much."*

Consequences as well as rewards

Every client we know has a rewards system. Yet, more than you would imagine have no system of consequences for team members not meeting expectations. Lombardi's players receiving the crisp bills for consistent level "two" performance and improvement felt prideful and honored. However, those with zeros on their report card knew there would be consequences.

Winning through preparation

We break down sales leadership into two fundamental components: skills and strategy. Lombardi's emphasis on grading film performance is an illustration of his emphasis on skills. He personally rode the blocking sled during practice.

He also thoroughly researched his opponent during the week. He would then involve his staff in developing the game plan, or strategy. With the skills honed through repetition and with the strategy set and communicated, there was little to do on the actual game day. In fact his players joked that, once the game started, he was the most useless guy on the sideline. On game day, it was up to them and they knew it.

Don't forget the basics

Lombardi once opened pre-season camp by holding up a ball and saying, "Gentleman, this is a football." To which team cut up Max McGee replied, "Can you slow down coach. You are going a little fast."

Never take yourself too seriously

Even Lombardi laughed at McGee's remark.

Your team will respect you for the stands you take

Lombardi was a native New Yorker. Born near Brooklyn, he went to college at Fordham where he was one of the legendary "Seven Blocks of Granite". He first coached at an area high school and then was an assistant at West Point. Lombardi broke in with the pros as an assistant with the New York Giants before taking over the reins at Green Bay.

On one of his first road trips with the Packers he encountered segregated housing and feeding arrangements for his players. When he returned to Green Bay, he personally visited every restaurant and tavern that had a reputation for segregation. His message was clear. Discriminate against any Packer and the place would be off limits to all Packers. On the next southern road trip he used his West Point connections to make arrangements for the entire team to stay at a local army base.

Know when to change the plays

When Lombardi came to the New York Giants he introduced an offense that had been successful at West Point. Old pros like Charlie

Connerly and gifted new ones like Frank Gifford could not hide their skepticism. Rather than jamming it down their throats, he visited with them in their pre-season residence hall rooms and asked for their help. He earned their respect and loyalty and the Giant's offense became one of the best in the league.

Know when to make personnel changes

Packer center Jim Ringo brought an agent with him to his annual contract conference with Lombardi. The agent pushed Lombardi for a raise for his client. Lombardi excused himself from his office. When he returned a few minutes later he said, "Take it up with the Eagles. I just traded Mr. Ringo to them."

Teamwork

Following a rare loss, Lombardi gathered his team around him and said, *"Let it be an example to all of us. The Green Bay Packers are no better than anyone else when they aren't ready, when they play as individuals and not as one . . . Our greatest glory is not in never falling, but in rising every time we fall."*

Winning

Selling and football are two fields where there are winners and losers. Perhaps the most famous saying attributed to Lombardi is, *"Winning isn't everything. It is the only thing."* Maraniss provides a fairly extensive treatment of the origin of that quote. It was actually uttered by a young actress playing a football coach's daughter. Lombardi saw the movie and, sure it hung on the locker room walls of the Packers. But, the saying appeared at other NFL camps as well.

What about this emphasis on winning? Critics have said it has been over emphasized. My take on Lombardi and winning is that his real emphasis was on "playing to win." There is a subtle but important difference. Lombardi wasn't the kind of coach who berated his team after they lost. He would, in fact be a consoling influence. Before long, he would be looking ahead to prepare for the next game, or even season. He surprised his players by how quickly he tried to lighten the mood after a loss.

Ever catch yourself or your team going through the motions instead of playing to win? Playing to win means recognizing that your objective is to win the game, or the account, by executing the best skills and strategy each and every time.

Perhaps Paul Hornung put it best in a letter he wrote to his coach once his playing days had ended. *"I believe the greatest thing I learned from your Football has not only been the idea of winning but WHY you want to win."*

And, the WHY is winning instills pride. *"Everybody has ability, but pride in performance is what makes the difference. Now, how do you develop pride? Pride is developed from a winning tradition."*

When Pride Still Mattered by David Maraniss. Does pride still matter in your team?

Summary

Are there any leaders among us who couldn't improve their performance by:

- Knowing your players
- Using different motivational strategies for different players
- Using rewards that fit the culture
- Rendering consequences as well as rewards
- Preparing strategy and emphasizing skills
- Emphasizing the basics
- Remembering not to take yourself too seriously

- Taking important stands
- Knowing when to change the plays
- Knowing when to change the players
- Promoting teamwork
- And, playing to win

Sales Management Diagnosis: September 1998

One of the consulting services we provide is a diagnosis of broken or under performing sales organizations. We employ a rather eclectic model that we have developed to guide our investigation. It is one that sales managers can use anytime they are scratching their heads and wondering, "Now, why isn't this sales team delivering like it should?" We organize our approach around the following six management considerations: Expectations, Rewards, Consequences, Tools, Skills & Knowledge, & Assignment.

1) Expectations The sales manager was wondering why his team was not making the expected number of weekly sales calls. We asked the sales reps. Their answer: *"Nobody told us how many calls we were supposed to make. Yeah, we can do that."*

We always start our investigation of what's broke by checking to see if expectations are clear. Often, they are not. Step One in effective sales force management is to be absolutely clear on what you expect. This is an instance where both oral and written communications are appropriate. It is Step One because it should start as early as recruitment and selection.

2) Rewards She was a young star. Six figure income performer. Despite her success, she left her organization. " I almost begged them for recognition. They thought dollars did everything. It didn't."

SST Seller Profiles will guide you in how to deliver those crucial rewards when expectations are met, and especially when they are exceeded. Recognizing that the "Feelings" preferred star described above wanted recognition would have saved her, and all the costs associated with replacing her. Retaining talent is always cheaper than recruiting it.

Incidentally, I agree with Steven Covey on the damaging effects of ranking members of a sales team. Research reported in The Hay Group's <u>People, Pay & Performance</u> (see p. 147 "Dangling Carrots") shows that these contests actually have an adverse impact on performance. As Covey points out, we want more than one winner on a sales team.

3) <u>Consequences</u> The son of the owner, who made it clear that he didn't like sales anyway, routinely arrived at the weekly sales meeting late and unprepared. Predictably, others began to show-up late and under prepared for the meeting as well.

Rendering consequences for failing to meet expectations can be tricky. Human nature is such that we postpone unpleasant tasks. However, if you don't confront a team member who falls short on expectations others are satisfying, your <u>consequence</u> will be an under performing team. If it goes unchecked, undesirable behavior will spread like a virus.

Nobody likes being reprimanded in public, even when they deserve it. Always praise in public and criticize in private.

4) <u>Tools</u> We differentiate between *"Tools"* and *"Skills"*. A carpenter applies his *"skills"* when using the *"tools"* in his box: hammers, saws, screwdrivers, squares, etc.

What we sometimes find is that management invests heavily in the latest selling "tool" but neglects to provide selling "skills". The biggest culprits of this phenomenon have been brought to us by the marvels of technology.

"Let's get everyone a neat new notebook computer, load it with the latest whiz bang contact management system, sit back and watch sales zoom."

While we have never seen this approach work, we have seen clients and potential clients pour princely sums into technology tools. By the time they have determined that their tools have not delivered the desired results, something new is on the market with shinier bells and louder whistles. Like to guess what happens next? Sadly, you are right.

I am not suggesting that tools are unimportant. They are, however, never a substitute for skills and knowledge.

5) Skills Some will break this category into "product knowledge" and "selling skills". Many who are under performing provide only the former. It is neat, clean and nearly every manufacturer offers training for its resellers, sometimes free.

Many managers cling to anachronistic views of selling believing balderdash like good sales people are born and not made. Others blindly trust numbers believing that, no matter what happens with those soft skills like consultative or relationship selling, making the requisite numbers of calls and reciting prepared scripts will produce the desired results. Even more devastating are organizations trusting that all experienced sales people already know how to sell.

Every time a sales person gets in front of a prospective or current client and does the wrong things an opportunity is lost. A common list of "wrong things" includes: a superficial investigation, prolonged preliminaries, handling objections, memorized closing scripts or asking questions that can only be answered "yes".

Investment in developing selling skills and knowledge will show returns many times over. Not only has SST demonstrated bottom line impact from a 500% increase with one client or a 200% jump with another, it plays a meaningful role in retention of sales talent. Helping those you manage learn and grow professionally are the surest ways to improve performance and to reduce attrition of high performers.

6) Assignment This is more than a euphemism for termination. Understanding personality types can be an essential management tool for arranging team selling. For example, "Thinkers" and "Feelers" have different natural antennae that can complement one another in team selling. Another application is to assign people to industry fields where their natural communication style is prevalent.

Summary You don't have to wait to get sick to benefit from this model. It can be helpful to stay well by performing regular assessments of how effective your management is in each of the six categories.

Dangling Carrots: September 1998

From time-to-time we assist client organizations in designing and implementing pay for performance incentive programs. Generally, it is upon discovering problems with "Rewards" when we conduct an assessment as described in the lead article.

Whenever I undertake a project of this nature I team-up with Dr. James Lakso who is an expert in such matters. Jim's day job is as Provost at Juniata College. Recently, Jim referred me to an excellent resource: *People, Pay & Performance* by Flannery et. al., Free Press, 1996.

A central tenet of this work is the importance of aligning pay incentive strategies with the unique needs of the organization: if you will, its culture. Put another way, an effective incentive program for one organization can fail miserably with another.

We help clients gain a comprehensive understanding of rewards.

We look at both extrinsic (salary, cash bonuses, "set of steak knives") and intrinsic rewards. The latter are less tangible, but often more powerful. They include personal and professional growth, belonging, recognition and satisfaction from a job well done. To motivate people you need to do more than dangle carrots.

Paradox II: Soft Skills Make a Hard Difference: January 1999

"The good news", the CEO tells her new VP for sales and marketing, "is that you have 150 people working for you. The bad news is none of them know it."

Does this sound funny but true? Charles Handy (1995) suggests in The Age of Paradox that seemingly contradictory concepts guide modern management practices. Among them are the one faced by the new VP for sales: encourage autonomy in the work force while being accountable for their performance. Others include: act globally and locally at the same time; be planned yet flexible; cater to niches while being a mass marketer; and emphasize both teamwork and independent thinking. Successful modern businesses, he asserts, reconcile the contradictions rather than choose between them.

In an earlier newsletter (November, 1997, p. 113), I wrote about "SST & SPIN: A Paradox". On the surface it seems that SPIN should be easier than SST. Paradoxically, however, our field research consistently shows that the steps and tools comprising SST are easier to master and use than SPIN. Asking good questions simply requires more practice and discipline than relating to clients in their preferred communication style.

This article treats yet another business paradox we have discovered: **Soft skills make a hard difference.** The formulation of this paradox is based on our experiences helping clients in diverse industries: from information technology, to windows and doors, to prescription benefit managers to kosher poultry to higher education.

Perhaps it is not surprising that the issues our clients confront are more similar than they are different. They all want to sell on value rather than compete in the market as a commodity.

Most seek to distinguish their products or services with so-called hard differentiators. One will go to market with a shinier bell. Meanwhile, the competition has researched and developed a louder whistle. Then, it is left to the poor sales staff to position themselves with prospective clients on the relative features, advantages and benefits of shinier bells or louder whistles. While the research and development guys think it is the break through of the century, prospective clients respond with dreaded "MEGO". (This is the acronym for "My Eyes Glaze Over")

The crucial element that is often left out of the "hard differentiators" approach to sales and marketing is the client. Mike Morucci, sales director of Penn State Geisinger Health Plan, summed up what he called the central tenet of SST, "It is not about *you*. It is about *them*." Once we are able to translate Mike's contribution to Latin, we will use it as the official SST motto.

Rackham's (1988) research shows that the introduction of hard differentiators is typically met with a decline in sales performance. This is because most sales people pitch them more and seek to understand less. Pitching hard differentiators actually drives clients further away.

We have learned that the best way to sell value is through so called "soft skills". It begins with a focus, not on "hard differentiators" but on "them", the clients. Excellent questions, asked the right way, are soft skills that are essential to understanding the client. The second essential SST skill is planning and implementing strategies for multiple buying influences in the account. Miller & Heiman (1998) have called them economic, user and technical buyers. Last, but definitely not least, selling on value requires communicating effectively with the buyers in their (not your) preferred style.

Hard differentiators like shinier bells and louder whistles fail to produce hard results. Pitching them puts the focus on "you" and not on "them". The soft differentiators of "asking the right question right", listening, and communicating in the preferred style of your client puts the focus where it belongs: on the client. Paradoxically, soft differentiators, and not hard ones, produce hard results.

Silver Bullets: September 1998

Return with me to the days of yesteryear when a brave man of justice fought to right the wrongs in a land known as Texas. He wore a mask to disguise his identity from the bad guys who believed they had killed him in a cowardly ambush. Accompanied by his faithful Indian companion, Tonto, the Lone Ranger chose as his signature . . . the Silver Bullet.

"Silver Bullet" has become a management metaphor for correcting a problem with a single, expensive shot. Often they miss the target. Such is the case with sales organizations relying on psychological tests in screening for selection.

I know of what I speak. My doctoral dissertation included a cross validation of a psychological test and "Tests and Measurement" is a course I taught at the college level.

If you are using a test for selection purposes, you should become familiar with a document titled, "Uniform Guidelines for Employee Selection Procedures" It was developed jointly by the friendly folks at the Departments of Justice and Labor, the Civil Service Commission and the Equal Opportunity Commission.

Fundamentally, you will need to ensure that the instrument is valid and that it does not exert an adverse impact on women and minorities. This kind of validity is the predictive variety which can only be reported in empirical terms. The following are not acceptable as validity indicators: *"all forms of promotional literature; data bearing on the frequency of a procedure's usage; testimonial statements and credentials of sellers, users, or consultants; and other non empirical or anecdotal accounts of selection practices or selection outcomes."*

While there are instruments available that satisfy federal guidelines for employee selection, many I have come across don't even come close. So, Ke-mo sah-bee, if you are afraid you might fire a "Silver Bullet" right into your foot, give me a call and I will provide you with a free assessment of your current assessment. Hi-Yo, Silver, Away!

Kirkpatrick's Model: July 1998

We have an interesting mix of clients using SST ranging from Fortune 100 firms to small professional practices with one or two partners focusing on business development. For those of you in training departments with large organizations, reference to the Kirkpatrick model for evaluation is as elementary as ABC (I don't mean always be closing). However, for readers in firms too small for a dedicated training department, Kirkpatrick's model is one you should know about.

Kirkpatrick is one of those enviable guys who parlayed his dissertation into a career. He introduced his model in the late 50s and today it is the standard by which organizations evaluate training. What I like about the Kirkpatrick model is the utter common sense that it makes.

Level one is "Reaction". This is where most training evaluations start and end. How did the participants react to the training? Did they like it? By themselves, favorable reactions and smiling faces are not enough. Kirkpatrick's level two examines "Learning" new skills or acquiring new knowledge.

Rackham has observed that the requisite question in evaluating a sale-straining program is "Do people use it?" Pardon the pun, but this is a different SPIN, on Kirkpatrick's level three where changes in "Behavior" are assessed. It is not sufficient for training participants to have liked the program and to have learned something. They need to behave differently.

Finally, level four looks at results. Did the training deliver EVA, or add economic value to the organization.

For some kinds of training, like team building, gathering quantifiable data at level four is difficult. That's not the case for sales training. Here the acid test should be improved sales performance, quantifiable in the number of new accounts as well as in dollars.

SST has built in assessment mechanisms at all four levels. We would be delighted to work with you to construct a four level assessment. It is the only way to know that the training you are providing is delivering the results you want and need.

Rackham & Gates See Similar Future: August 1999

It is always intriguing when two well-regarded observers study a question from very different perspectives and arrive at very similar conclusions. This is the case with Neil Rackham (1999) Rethinking the Sales Force and Bill Gates (1999) with Business at the Speed of Thought. The question these two leaders examine is the nature of selling and buying in the new market place.

Regular readers of this newsletter need no introduction to Neil Rackham. He is the pioneer who brought substance and science to consultative selling. It was his research that established the importance of asking good questions and debunked the then traditional sales approaches that emphasized clever closing scripts.

Unless you have been living in a cave for the last ten years, you know who Bill Gates is. He's the guy who co-founded Microsoft and is, by most accounts, the richest man in the world. Never mind that the federal government believes he acquired his fortune by using unfair business practices. (*Gates is so powerful that I fear that criticism during Microsoft's antitrust suit could result in all my Microsoft software products crashing. After all, if they can reset my computer clock when we move to Daylight Savings Time, why couldn't they erase my files?*)

One of Rackham's central points in Rethinking the Sales Force is that modern customers are changing the way they make buying decisions. Three distinct buying modes (transactional, consultative and enterprise) have evolved and the way to add value for customers is different for each.

Transactional purchases are made when the buyer already knows everything he or she needs to know about the product or service. Time spent with a sales person doesn't add value. In fact, it can even subtract value because transactional buyers resent wasting valuable time with someone asking them about what they already know and understand.

On the other hand, consultative buyers benefit from a sales person helping them understand the full nature of their problem. This is the kind of consultative sale where SST skills enable sales people to communicate effectively and build trusting relationships that are often more important than the product or service itself. Enterprise sales are the rarest variety and are made when sellers and buyers actually become partners.

Although at times it reads like a Microsoft commercial (*oops!*), Business at the Speed of Thought helps us understand the impact of technology on buying. Gates makes the case for the pervasiveness of technology. Soon most workers will use computers everyday. Personal computers will be in most households and homes and businesses will be connected through the World Wide Web. Electronic mail will be as common as telephone communication and preferred over paper or "snail" mail.

Inevitably, people will begin to, not only use, but prefer "digital" communication. It is easier and faster. I am an example. As a recent attendee of a college reunion, I was mildly annoyed that I couldn't register on-line. Paper mail would miss the deadline, and phone registration was long distance and time consuming.

Gates asserts that these trends will result in more-and-more transactions between businesses and customers being done electronically. A customer will visit a company's web site and order what he or she needs quickly and efficiently. The operative word in this paragraph is "transaction" which defines the first of Rackham's three buying modes.

Eventually competing businesses will have web pages and on-line catalogues that look very similar; like Amazon's and Barnes & Nobles. It will become increasingly difficult to differentiate one business from another for the commodity shopper. This is why commodity-buying decisions are often based on relatively small differences in price.

At the next buying levels (consultative and enterprise) however, value is added by the quality of human interaction between and among buyers and sellers. Price is often secondary to the trust the buyer has that the seller can deliver a solution. Customer service and sales will focus on high-value transactions.

Rackham looks at future through a sales and marketing lens and encourages businesses to organize their sales around the three buying modes. Gates looks at the "Road Ahead" (his 1995 title) and sees a similar future where Rackham's transactional buying mode will be catalyzed by technological growth.

Paradoxically, pervasive technology does not mean that human interaction will be less important. How sales and customer service people relate to clients will be of even greater strategic significance in the future. According to Gates, "Sales and customer service will become the primary value-added function in every business."

The key "Business Lessons" (as Gates calls them) from this article are to:

- ⇒ Recognize that adding value means different things to different buyers.
- ⇒ Have a web site that enables quick and efficient "transactional" purchases.
- ⇒ Have sales and customer service people who are skilled at building consultative relationships.

Chapter XIV

The SST Practice Tee

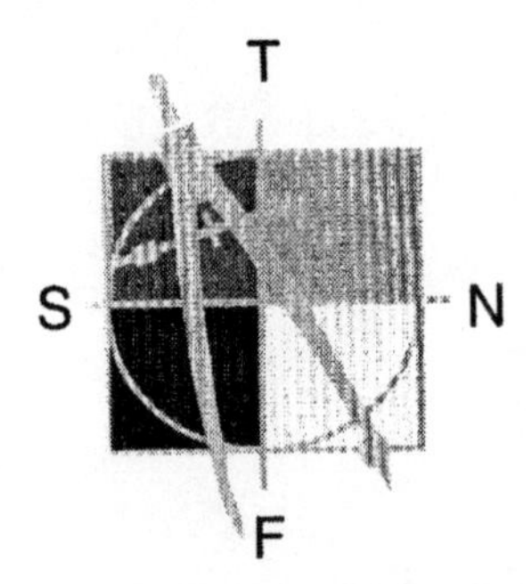

Back in the introduction, I indicated that this book was for those people who thought the SST concept sounded cool, but were uncertain how it was actually delivered. I hope we have answered that question.

However, there are other readers who will like to know how this powerful concept can be harnessed for their own, or their sales teams', performance. They are facing the "Knowing Doing Gap".

A recent book by that title (Pfeffer and Sutton, 2000) documents the billions of dollars firms spend on training every year that lead to little change in how people behave or how business gets conducted. They charge organizations with failing to provide means for people to bridge the gap from "knowing" to "doing". Frankly, it is an interesting treatise of what common sense already tells all us.

Our take is that, although organizations and consultants could certainly do a better job, there is only one person who can close the gap between "Knowing" and "Doing". No surprise: that person is you.

Ralph Waldo Emerson wrote, *"No man can learn what he has not preparation for learning."* If you are prepared to learn how to convert your knowledge of SST into results for you or your sales team, the remainder of this chapter is for you.

As a reformed educational psychologist, I could liberally sprinkle this piece with scientific references on how adults learn. Since that would bore most of you out of your skulls, I have elected golf as our metaphor instead.

Let's say that you are frustrated with your game because you are giving up a lot of strokes around the green. You are hitting the ball off the tee and from fairway to green better than your playing partners. But, when you get near the hole, they are able to "get up and down" and take fewer strokes to finish the hole.

Tired of losing every weekend, you buy an instructional book on golf and go immediately to the chapters on pitching, chipping and putting. You recognize that your techniques are seriously flawed. Your hands are in the wrong position. Your stance is closed when it should be open. You must be decelerating. Your head must be moving.

Now you have pinpointed the problem areas and have a model to move from some of the bad practices to good ones. Would you expect better results without actually picking up a wedge and hitting some balls? Never.

Learning SST is perfectly analogous. The only way to get better performance results is to:

1. Practice it
2. Do it

The SST Practice Tee

Although it can certainly seem more difficult when you are hacking your way around the course, golf fundamentally has three components: 1.) The grip 2.) The stance and 3.) The swing.

SST can also be broken down into three skill areas: 1.) Questioning 2.) Listening 3.) Balance & Shade

Questioning

On the practice tee, we are going to begin with questioning drills. Refer to Chapter Three on "The Investigation".

Role Play Your Line of Investigation Drill.

- Choose questions that fit you the best from the four categories (Facts, Problems, Consequences, What if)
- Choose three family members, friends or colleagues to role play a prospect
- Ask them to critique your questioning
    - o Did they think they were good questions?
    - o Did they feel that you were listening?
    - o Did you start to build rapport?
    - o Would they trust you as a solution provider?
- Write down what they say to help you make comparisons
- Compare what your role play interviewees offer
- Look for common themes
- Modify your list into your "Line of Investigation"

Anticipate Objections with Questions Drill.

- Reread pages 44 & 45 on "Objections as Symptoms"
- Write down all the objections you have heard in your last five calls

- When you complete a call, start making notes on the objections you hear
- High volume and broad topics suggest that you are pitching prematurely and truncating the investigation
- If your symptoms are high volume and broad topics, go back and do Drill One again
- If you consistently hear one objection you may be able to create value with better questions
- Write down the objections
- Scratch your head (On the SST Practice Tee this is analoous to waggling the club head) and ask, "What is behind this objection?"
- Often, we find prospects "objecting to investing" and gambling with what they have
- List all the problems and consequences they might have with their current situation
- What could go wrong with their gamble?
- Convert the list of what could go wrong into questions
- Here's an illustration from a client representing computer networks (Local Area Networks or LANs)
    - Walk me through what happened the last time the network went down
    - What jobs were scheduled to get done that day?
    - How did they get done?
    - Any deadlines missed?
    - Did you have to pay overtime that day?
    - Did non-exempt staff have to stay late or come in during the evenings?
    - Who was involved in finding a solution?
    - What could they have been doing if they weren't putting out this fire?
    - What did it mean to your customers or clients?
    - Have you been losing any?
    - How is morale when the network goes down?

- Ever lose someone who took a lateral position that had better IT support?
- Did you ever assign a dollar value to what it costs when the network goes down?
- We have, and for an organization comparable to yours it averages $XXX.
- What would a more reliable LAN mean to reaching your objectives?

Listening

The biggest deficiency we observe with investigation skills is with listening. Asking a terrific question and then not listening to the answer is a wasted exercise. Yet, we see this pattern committed over-and-over.

Those of you who have participated in SST know that we conduct a listening exercise called "The Three Stage Rocket". Participants are assigned to groups of three and assigned a topic to debate. For example, one person will argue for no speed limit on interstate highways. Another will be in favor of maintaining a 55 MPH limit. The third person moderates and enforces the "Three Stage Rocket Rule", which is:

Before you can make your point, you must restate what you just heard to the satisfaction of the person who said it.

What we soon realize with this exercise is that we don't listen. We reload. Instead of trying to understand the other person we are preparing what we are going to say next. It is extremely difficult to listen effectively when we are reloading.

When we process the exercise we will also ask the participants how it felt when someone started listening instead of reloading. You already know the most common responses: "Terrific" and "Unusual".

For those of you who are Steven Covey fans you will recognize this as seeking to understand before we seek to be understood. Neil Rackham refers to it as shifting from persuading to understanding. Carl Rogers called it being client centered. The concept is so central to SST that is the basis for our Latin motto: *Non de nobis agitur sed de istis.* It is not about you. It is about them.

Whatever model you prefer the lesson is abundantly clear, you cannot understand your client without listening to him or her. Still, becoming a good listener is a challenging task. It often requires overcoming many years of bad communication habits like reloading when we should be listening.

The Three-Stage Rocket (TSR) Drill.

- The next time you are dealing with some disagreement practice the Three Stage Rocket Rule
- Say, "Before I tell you my position on this, I first want to listen to you. Why don't you start and once you have made your case, I will restate to make sure that I understand. Then, it will be your turn to listen to me."
- This drill is excellent with spouses and significant others. It also can be practiced with friends in the context of "light" differences of opinion like: favorite authors, vacation spots, airlines, restaurants, movies, athletic teams etc.
- Be active with a partner and practice the TSR rule and critique how well one another is listening.
- Apply the skills you learn from these drills to your next sales call
- Next time you encounter some real conflict you may want to propose the TSR Rule

Balance & Shade

For the Balance & Shade exercises we presume that you have a good comfort level with your four-letter code and understand the

SST model as it has been outlined through out the book. Through the Balance & Shade drills we seek to improve your skills at: 1.) Recognizing type preferences in others and; 2.) Determining which messages in your products value proposition are S, N, T or F.

Celebrity Profiling Drill

- If you are an Extravert, this drill can be more fun when you do it with another person or with a group of people familiar with SST, the Myers Briggs Type Indicator or Jungian theory.
- Pick a celebrity and go through the Behavioral Cues in Chapter Two, SST Tools
- What do you think his or her four-letter code is?
- If you want to make it a competition, you can visit www.mbtypeguide.com which is an online resource that can link you to resources that have typed a wide array of celebrities. Here are a few: Winston Churchill (ENTP); Elvis (ESFP); Colin Powell (ESTJ); Hillary Clinton (ENTJ); Jacqueline Onassis (ISFP); Albert Einstein (INTP); Joan of Arc (INFP)
- Read the corresponding Buyer Profile in Chapters Five through Eight

Type Watching Drill

- This is a first cousin to Celebrity Profiling and uses the same SST Tool, Behavioral Cues
- The chief distinction is that we are not necessarily typing celebrities, just people we know well
- Start with the people you live with
- How do you see them on each of the four scales?
- How do they see themselves?
- How do they see you?
- How do you see yourself?

- Discuss the Buyer Profiles in Chapters Five through Eight. Would they be a good road map to communicate effectively with the various personality types you encounter?

Balanced Messages Drill

- Pick up all representative promotional literature your firm uses
- Pull out the last three proposals, presentations or pitches you made
- Examine these materials against "Implications of the Four Part Framework" in Chapter Two
- Take each theme and determine whether it is S, N, T or F.
- Here are some hypothetical themes to give you a sense of what to look for:
    - Sensing Illustration: *"ABC Company was founded in 1928 and today employs 3,518 staff in 18 countries"*
    - Intuitive Illustration: *" The only thing certain in today's economy is change. ABC empowers you to make it"*
    - Thinking Theme: *"Your investment in an ABC solution will be returned many times over."*
    - Feeling Theme: *"At ABC we take our corporate citizen ship seriously. Last year our partnership with the "Save the River Foundation" helped reduce the level of pollution in our river and improve conditions for the marine life that inhabit it.*
- How balanced are your messages? Typically, this exercise indicates far more Sensing and Thinking themes than Intuitive and Feeling ones.
- Make a list of Sensing, Intuitive, Thinking and Feeling Themes.

Implementing SST
Taking it from the Practice Tee to the Course

Every golfer knows that moving from the practice tee to the course is an important step in improving your game. Similarly, while doing the practice drills outlined above will help build skills and confidence, it is not enough. You will need to "bring it to the course".

Behavioral Cues of Existing Clients or Prospects. The best place to start is with the "Type Watching Drill". Progressively, we have moved from typing celebrities to the people you live with. By now you should have a pretty good comfort level with both the SST model and the Behavioral Cues tool.

The next step is to use the Behavioral Cues with a client or prospect with whom you have had some dealings. What do you see? Can you identify all four preferences?

Study the corresponding Buyer Profile. Does it sound like a good match? If there are one or more scales you are unclear on, read the closest profiles. For example, if the prospect clearly shows EST behaviors but you are unsure of the J and P scale, read both the ESTJ and ESTP profiles.

Behavioral Cues of New Clients or Prospects. Rule number one here is not to type during the call. Focus on the client by asking good questions and listening. In practice it is pretty common for a prospect to "scream" his or her preferences. In fact, we go into the call with a working hypothesis informed by Industrial Profiles outlined in Chapter Two.

If, for example, we are meeting with the CFO whom we know from our Advocate has a background in accounting, we would be entertaining a ST hypothesis. If she displays classic ST behavior during the interview *("How much? What are the steps? Proven with clients like us?")* it is fine to make and confirm the ST association.

Then, file it away until after the interview. During the interview focus on her and be a TSR listener. Make sure you understand her and her organizations business problems as thoroughly as you can.

Balance. Let's say that you are planning a presentation to a buying committee. It may even be a "Beauty Contest" where four contestants have been asked to present. The appropriate SST behavior is to "Balance" your presentation.

Return to the "Balanced Messages Drill" or the "SST Theme Bank" we delivered following working with you as a client. Review what you plan to present. Is it balanced?

The tendency we find in reviewing both written and verbal presentations is for them to be out of balance and leaning toward the preferences of the presenter and those of his or her culture.

Shade. Lets pick up the CFO illustration described four paragraphs above. The ST hypothesis is clearly confirmed. Further, her Extraverted preference was clearly demonstrated. You asked one question and she answered eight others you had planned. Then, toward the end of the interview she proposed specific follow-up steps with corresponding deadlines. If there ever was an ESTJ, she is it.

Shading our messages means leading with Sensing and Thinking themes. It does not mean sending only and ST messages however. There are two reasons for this: First, most capable and intellectually mature decision makers have learned to use all four mental functions, much the way a tennis player has learned to hit forehands and backhands. They just prefer one over the other.

Second, many decisions require the involvement of more than one person. This is where the Miller & Heiman buyer influence model (Chapter Nine) comes into play. Our ESTJ CFO may be gathering information to deliver to an INFP CEO. She might prefer a ball hit to her forehand but knows that her CEO prefers backhands.

ILD

The key to learning any skill, including SST, is to:

1. Practice it
2. Do it

SST Training

If you are interested in learning more about SST training you can visit our website at www.tildenSST.com. There you will find information on how to contact us as well as a list of clients we have served. Thank you

References on Personality Type

Macdaid, G. P., McCaulley, M.H., Kainz, R. I. *Atlas of Type Tables*, Gainesville, FL, CAPT, 1986 de Laszlo, V., *The Basic Writings of Carl Jung*, New York, Random House, 1959

Myers, I. B., & Briggs, P. B., *Gifts Differing*, Palo Alto, CA, Consulting Psychologists Press, Inc., 1993

Kummerow, J. M., & Hirsch, S., *Life Types*, New York, Warner Books, 1989

Kummerow, J. M., Burger, N. J. & Kirby, L. K., *Work Types*, New York, Warner Books, 1997

Lawrence, G., *People Types and Tiger Stripes*, Gainesville, FL, CAPT, 1993

References on SST, SPIN & Strategic Selling

Heiman, S. E., Sanchez, D., Tuleda, T., *The New Strategic Selling*, New York, Warner Books, 1997

Rackham, N., *Spin Selling*, New York, McGraw-Hill, 1988

Rackham, N., *Major Account Sales Strategy*, New York, McGraw-Hill, 1989

Rackham, N., Friedman, L. & Ruff, R., *Managing Major Sales*,

New York, Harper Business, 1991

Rackham, N., Friedman, L. & Ruff, R., *Getting Partnering Right,* New York, McGraw-Hill, 1996

Rackham, N. & DeVincentis, J., *Rethinking the Sales Force*, New York, McGraw-Hill, 1999

Tilden, A., *SST Newsletter Articles archived at www.tildensst.com*

63-TILD

BVG